OUR LORD JESUS CHRIST
A Plant of Renown

Our Lord Jesus Christ
A Plant of Renown

Leonard Sheldrake

Foreword by William MacDonald

Gospel Folio Press
304 Killaly St. West Port Colborne, ON L3K 6A6

OUR LORD JESUS CHRIST: A PLANT OF RENOWN
by Leonard Sheldrake
First printing 1950

Published by Gospel Folio Press
304 Killaly St.
West Port Colborne, ON L3K 6A6

ISBN 1-882701-16-X

Cover design by J. B. Nicholson, Jr.

Printed in the United States of America

Christ possessed by faith here is young heaven and glory in the bud.

—SAMUEL RUTHERFORD

Contents

Foreword

Horatius Bonar once said that Samuel Rutherford had

A thirst no earthly stream could satisfy;
A hunger that must feed on Christ or die.

To all who share this thirst and hunger, the following pages will prove a feast of good things. The book will endear itself to those who love our Lord Jesus Christ because it is all about Him. It is filled with great thoughts about the Saviour. It is filled with exalted expressions of worship and appreciation of the One who is supremely worthy.

Some of Mr. Sheldrake's vintage will recognize portions of the book as messages delivered by the author at various times throughout his ministry. All such will welcome the preservation of these addresses in more permanent form. It is hoped that as they read these pages, they will once again recapture the sound of a voice that throbbed with emotion for God—a voice that had tears in it.

No one ever reads a book without being affected in some way by it. As the reader beholds the glory of the Lord in this volume, may he be changed into the same image from glory to glory, even as by the Spirit of the Lord.

—WILLIAM MACDONALD

Introduction

My grandfather was a small businessman, active father, and committed shepherd of God's people. He was a busy man. He took his fair share from the critic's lash and more than his share of life's burdens. What I admired most about him was that he never became cynical or bitter through the dark times of life. He told me one of his secrets: he read this book once a year, "because," he said, "it keeps my soul sweet."

We have also come to appreciate the warm devotion of Leonard Sheldrake's written ministry and wish to re-introduce it to a new generation of readers who want to love their Lord the way He deserves. *The Plant of Renown* is suited to help you do just that.

To make the book even more useful, we have added a scripture index and an appendix listing the names and titles of Christ with references.

An anonymous writer has penned these words for our encouragement: "We may speak of Him as much as we wish, and praise Him to the bound of our capacity without ever being reprimanded by Heaven for exaggerating His excellencies." May the Spirit of the Lord, who delights to take from the "things of Christ" and show them to us, bring forth this sweet fruit in our lives, the kind of fruit that can only come from abiding in this Plant of Renown.

—THE PUBLISHER

11

Preface

One of the characteristics of the last days is the abounding iniquity of the wicked. The effect of this iniquity on the people of God is to make their love grow cold. "Because iniquity shall abound, the love of many shall wax cold" (Mt. 24:12).

When love to Christ should be warmest it is liable to be coldest. Just before we meet the Lord in the air it seems to be easiest to forget Him. How sad if love should fail just before the marriage supper of the Lamb!

The meditations contained in this book are written to warm the hearts of the people of God in view of our Lord's return. These messages on the person of our Lord Jesus Christ are the fruit of years of exercise on this most absorbing theme. They are not cleverly written but they breathe the spirit of the writer; it is hoped they will lead the spirits of the readers to adoration and worship of Him who is the grand subject of all Scripture.

Those whose faith and love are strengthened by reading this book would do well to put it into the hands of others who need another vision of the One who is "altogether lovely."

—LEONARD SHELDRAKE

CHAPTER ONE

The Planting of the Lord

Plants are renowned for their fruit; all fruit is from plants. Christ was God's plant of renown in fulfillment of the promise of Jehovah: "And I will raise up for them a plant of renown..." (Ezek. 34:29). He was that choice Vine whose fruit cheered both God and man (Jud. 9:13; see also Jn. 15:1-8). He is also the wheat that grew in God's field, to make the bread to strengthen man's heart (Ps. 104:15; see also Jn. 12:24). The fig tree was renowned for its sweetness, and the upright palm for its luscious dates. The cedar of Lebanon was renowned for its majesty, and even the hyssop that sprang out of the wall had its own renown as the agent in the hand of the priest sprinkling precious blood on the leper to make him clean (Lev. 14:7).

All the fruit that ever grew, or herbs for the service of man, must be united into one volume of preciousness to present the glory and grace of Christ; who was raised up for us, as well as for Israel, to be God's plant of renown.

Plants are also renowned for their fragrance. The myrrh tree, the lign-aloe and the cassia tree produced those spices to make Messiah's garments fragrant in the ivory palaces. "All thy garments smell of myrrh and aloes and cassia, out of the ivory palaces whereby they have made thee glad" (Ps. 45:8).

Our Lord was renowned for His fragrance in the world where men's mouths were open sepulchers and our tongues had used deceit. His mouth was most sweet, and His lips dropped sweet-smelling myrrh, where every imagination of the thoughts of our hearts was only evil continually (Gen. 6:5). Our Lord did the loveliest deeds in the most lovely way. Some give without cheer-fulness, but not the Lord Jesus; the love of friends is often mixed with dissimulation, but not His love. His kindness was lov-ingkindness, and His mercy tender mercy. When He cleansed the leper He touched him; when He showed grace to the woman in the temple (Jn. 8) He did not desire to hear the details of the story of her shame. When the Lord gives wisdom He does not upbraid us for our ignorance (Jas. 1:5); He does not scold because we know so little. The Lord Jesus always gave commen-dation before He administered reproof. His ways were full of love, joy, peace, longsuffering, gentleness, goodness, faith, meekness, and temperance.

The soul of our Lord was like the Holy of Holies where the cherubim stretched their wings above the mercy seat, and where the fragrance of the incense was a continual delight. His life was like a garden, where springtime beauty in the flowers "gives a good smell." He was renowned for His lovely words and loving deeds. There never was one like the Lord Jesus whose days, like Canaan, flowed with milk and honey. No person might make a confection to smell like that used in the tabernacle (Ex. 30:38) for that fragrance was typical of Christ and no loveliness was ever lovely like His. There was only one such tender plant (Isa. 53:2) and He was cut off out of the land of the living. Solomon in all his glory was not arrayed like the lily of the field; but all the beauty of all the flowers, and all their fragrance, too, would not suffice to tell how altogether lovely He is.

"I will raise up for them a plant of renown," the Lord declared. It was for them. It was for us. When He was raised up in the house of David it was to save His people from their sins (Mt. 1:21). When He was raised up in resurrection it was to give repentance and remission of sins (Acts 5:31).

How marvelously His renown will be known on that glad day when He comes to be glorified in His saints and to be admired in all them that believe! Then the earth itself will be filled with "the knowledge of the Lord" (Isa. 11:9).

The plant of renown was raised up! That Holy Thing that was born of Mary was called the Son of God. Without the stain of man's corruption and beyond the reach of the curse on Solomon's seed, a Son and Heir was raised up to David to be for

Israel a plant of renown.

Plants are renowned as well for their beauty. Our Lord is the Rose of Sharon and the Lily of the Valley. He was thought of as commonplace and ordinary, but when examined, He is fragrant and beautiful like the rose, and pure and lovely like the lily. All the beauty of the light grows in the flowers of earth. This beauty is from light absorbed in the living processes of organic growth. Life in its most beautiful manifestation in the tender plants that grow feeds its soul on the light and displays its beauty to God and men. This was the moral glory of Christ, God's plant of renown. He is altogether lovely to the anointed eyes of His people and raptures the heart of God till He opens heaven to exclaim, "This is my beloved Son in whom I am well pleased."

He was a tender plant (Isa. 53:2) growing up before the Lord, an exotic, a plant from another land. He was native to another climate. He had been always admired and worshiped in heaven. Here He was unknown and unnoticed. "The world knew Him not." Except for God's protection, the tender plant would have been trodden down and destroyed.

There was a renown that was all His own in those tender years because He was content to be lowly and silent without renown in the world His hands had fashioned. It was a matter of new renown to Him that He who had been so honored and renowned in heaven should be altogether without renown in this cold, barren world. Lovely lowliness was never so altogether lovely as when the King of kings was a carpenter in Nazareth. He whose glory had flooded the heavens walked unknown along the lanes of a despised village in Galilee. He who had been on the throne of God sat now on a rude bench in a cottage of the poorest of the people. He whose hand had arranged the stars in the firmament worked hard with saw and hammer to provide that coarse and scanty livelihood that fed the hungry mouths of the laboring poor. He in whom God found all His delight was never once recognized or known by those nearest to Him, His kinsman according to the flesh.

His hidden years are hidden manna for those who can rise to appreciate the perfect submission and lowliness of Christ our Lord in Nazareth. His spotless humanity was the dew upon which the food of angels came down from heaven to feed men on the earth with the bread of life. There is nothing more pure and lovely in this sin-spoiled earth than the drops of morning dew, upon which the manna is said to have come from heaven. The world itself could not contain the books that God could write about the preciousness and fragrant beauty of Him, of that one plant of renown that grew up before God on earthly soil. There was the renown of the Plant before it blossomed in a public ministry of grace and power.

God who gave the flowers gave His Son to be a plant of renown on earth that by it He might reveal the life of heaven. And as mentioned, life and light are the source of all the fragrant beauty of the garden, which brings such gladness to appreciative hearts. Like the herb of the field, He was for the service of man. Like the leaves of the tree, He was for the healing of the nations. Like the fruit of the vine, He cheered God and man. Like the myrrh, the aloe, the cassia, He grew and suffered and died to fill the presence of God and the joy of His people with the most delightful fragrance. Like the flowers appearing on the earth, His coming brought the springtime when the birds sing, and when He and His people could walk together in a fellowship that shall one day be unbroken and unending.

Our Lord showed early on that He understood His mission when, at the age of twelve, He stayed behind at Jerusalem. When Mary and Joseph found Him in the temple, His mother said, "Son, why hast thou thus dealt with us? Behold, thy father and I have sought thee sorrowing" (Lk. 2:48). He answered, "How is it that ye sought me? wist ye not that I must be about *my Father's* business" (Lk. 2:49)?

This experience was needed to revive in the soul of Mary the memory of His person as the Son of God. The commonplace in His life at Nazareth had dimmed in the soul of Mary and Joseph the realization of His exalted glory as Emmanuel. It seems that even His words then did not immediately have the desired effect. "They understood not the saying that He spake unto them." But of Mary it is written, "His mother kept all these sayings in her heart" (Lk. 2:48-51).

How strange that the perfect lowliness of Him who was God-over-all did not cause wonder, love, and praise. Instead, His meekness caused souls to lose the sense of His infinite greatness!

Those who saw only His poverty and lowliness, rejected with scorn His majesty and exaltation. Those who knew who He was and from where He came, wondered with great admiration at the grace that could constantly stoop so low. Those who saw His glory, full of grace and truth, treasured His words of love and peace. Christ then, and ever since, caused in the hearts of men either the deepest reverence and devotion or the blind abhorrence of derision and scorn.

There could be no middle ground; either He was the greatest wonder of the giving love of God, or else the most pitiable example of colossal pretension and blasphemous delusion. Any man who honestly faces the facts of Old Testament prophecy and type, with the facts of New Testament record in the Gospels and Acts, must exclaim in His presence like Thomas, "My Lord and my God." How any intelligent person can carry the Bible and be a stranger to the glory and grace of Christ is a confounding mystery to me. It is like the insensibility that walks beneath the stars and says there is no God. It is blindness of the heart, coupled, it would seem, with perversion of the will.

The renown of the world's rulers is in rising to heights of human glory and attainment from obscurity and poverty. The renown of our Lord is in descending from heights of glory and majesty to depths of human poverty and shame. Men are renowned for climbing to satisfy their passion for power and pleasure; He is renowned for coming down in grace to a path of meekness and mercy in love to others.

John, the beloved apostle, viewing the infinite subject of the person and work of Christ, felt like devoted scientists scanning the infinite reaches of the universe; he wrote, "The world itself could not contain the books that should be written" (Jn. 21:25).

Jewish rabbis who reject His Messiahship, Unitarians who reject His Godhead, and even educated infidels who reject His Deity, have all spoken well of the person and words of Jesus of Nazareth. How they can do this without comprehending the implications of their confessions is a mystery to me.

Rabbi Prof. Emil G. Hirsch, Ph.D., LL.D., wrote, "The Jews of every shade of religious belief do not regard Jesus in the light of Paul's theology. But the Gospel Jesus, the Jesus who teaches so superbly the principles of Jewish ethics, is revered by all the lib-

19

eral expounders of Judaism. His words are studied; the New Testament forms a part of Jewish literature. Among the great preceptors that have worked the truths of which Judaism is the historical guardian, none, in our estimation and esteem, takes precedence over the Rabbi of Nazareth."

Rabbi Kaufman Kokler, Ph.D., wrote, "His whole manner of teaching, the so-called Lord's Prayer, the Golden Rule, the code of ethics expounded for the elect ones in the Sermon on the Mount, no less than His miraculous cures, show Him to have been...a popular saint. But He was more than an ordinary teacher and healer of men. He went to the very core of religion and laid bare the depths of the human soul."

Why does Rabbi Hirsch reject Paul's theology? What does he mean? The Jesus that this learned rabbi could not accept is the Christ of 1 Corinthians 15:3-4, "Christ died for our sins according to the scriptures; and...He was buried, and...He rose again the third day according to the scriptures." Or the Christ of Romans 1:1-4, "Paul, a servant of Jesus Christ, called to be an apostle, separated unto the gospel of God...concerning His Son Jesus Christ our Lord, which was made of the seed of David according to the flesh; and declared to be the Son of God with power, according to the Spirit of holiness, by the resurrection from the dead."

Prof. Hirsch forgets that Jesus of Nazareth was hated, rejected, and crucified because He said He was the Son of God. Why is he willing to accept "the Gospel Jesus," while rejecting the Jesus of Paul's writings? Is there any difference between them? They are one and the same. Paul was martyred for preaching "the Gospel Jesus."

Is Jesus not called "Christ," and "Son of God," and "Lord," in the Gospels? Do the Gospel writers not bear witness to His resurrection from the dead? When Paul was an unconverted rabbi, he hated Jesus of Nazareth because He said He was the Son of God. This was the kernel of the conflict at Jerusalem over Jesus of Nazareth for more than three years; His disciples and He Himself said He was the Christ. The rabbis then were no different from the rabbis today. They shut their eyes so that they could not see; they closed their ears so that they could not hear; they tried by deceit and persecution to squelch the testimony to

Christ's resurrection. They dared not question the disciples concerning stealing His body from the tomb. When all those who paid the soldiers to circulate this report had the disciples in the temple before them, why did they not bring up the serious charge of breaking the Roman seal and stealing His body?

Why will the rabbis of today not face the testimony of the Old Testament scriptures to Christ? These scriptures witness that the Christ would be the Son of God. They plainly told that He would be rejected and put to death by His own people. The resurrection of Christ is plainly revealed in the Psalms, and it is surely inferred in Isaiah 53: "Who shall declare his generation? for he was cut off out of the land of the living...he shall see his seed...He shall see of the travail of his soul, and shall be satisfied" (Isa. 53:8, 10-11).

How can Rabbi Kokler extol the Sermon on the Mount, yet not believe that Jesus was God? There was nothing more holy than the Law written on the tables of stone. In that Sermon on the Mount, Jesus of Nazareth did not hesitate to quote the Law and then say, "But I say unto you." A mere man would not have dared to do this. "Ye have heard that it hath been said, Thou shalt love thy neighbor, and hate thine enemy. But I say unto you, Love your enemies, bless them that curse you, and pray for them which despitefully use you and persecute you" (Mt. 5:43-44). In the end of the Sermon, Jesus of Nazareth said, "Many will say to Me in that day, Lord, Lord, have we not prophesied in Thy name?...and in Thy name done many wonderful works? And then will I profess unto them, I never knew you: depart from Me ye that work iniquity" (Mt. 7:22-23).

Who is this Man who prophesies that in the last day when sinners are brought to judgment they will call Him Lord? Who is this man who dares to picture Himself as Judge of all? Is He a mere man who takes the words of God into His lips and says, "Depart from Me, ye that work iniquity"?

Yet this is the Jesus of the Gospels; this is the Jesus of the Beatitudes; this is the Jesus of the Golden Rule. If He were not God He was a blasphemer. But He was not a blasphemer; He was "The Truth," and all His words were true. If His words were true, He was the One whose name is, "Wonderful, Counselor, *The Mighty God,* the Everlasting Father, the Prince of

Peace." He was David's Lord as well as David's son: "The Lord said unto my Lord, Sit Thou at My right hand, until I make Thine enemies Thy footstool" (Ps. 110:1).

The angels called Him Lord when He was born: "Unto you is born this day in the city of David a Saviour, which is Christ the Lord" (Lk. 2:11). The disciples called Him Lord with His commendation during His life, "Ye call me Master and Lord: and ye say well; for so I am" (Jn. 13:13). The dying thief called Him Lord when hanging on the cross, "Lord, remember me when Thou comest into Thy kingdom" (Lk. 23:42). Thomas called Him Lord in resurrection: "My Lord and my God" (Jn. 20:28).

The One who taught His disciples to pray, "Our Father which art in heaven" continually referred to God as "My Father." He said, "I and My Father are one" (Jn. 10:30) and, "As the Father knoweth Me, even so know I the Father" (Jn. 10:15). The Jews took up stones to stone Him because He said God was His Father; as they said, "Thou being a man, makest Thyself God." They did not stone Him because He *was* God.

How can the rabbis accept the Jesus of the Mount of Olives and reject the Christ of prophecy? Was Christ not declared to be more than a man? The prophecies foretold His coming as a man of the tribe of Judah and of the house of David. But the prophecies bore abundant witness to Christ's equality with God.

In the very first prophecy of the coming One, God Himself intimated that though the coming Messiah would be a man, He would be more than a man. In the garden of Eden, God said to the Serpent who was the author of the ruin on Adam and Eve, "I will put enmity between thee and the woman, and between thy seed and her Seed; it shall bruise thy head, and thou shalt bruise His heel" (Gen. 3:15).

The coming One would be a man, for He was to be the woman's seed: but He would be more than a man, for He would conquer Adam's conqueror. Why did God not say, "Adam's seed"? Why the seed of the woman, if not for virgin birth?

And Michael, the greatest of the angels, dare not bring against the devil a railing accusation, but said, "The Lord rebuke thee" (Jude 9). This One who is a man, for He has a heel, is mightier than Michael, for He bruised Satan's head.

David in Psalm 45 calls Him a man, for He is anointed with

the oil of gladness above His fellows (v. 7). Yet in verse 6 this One whom God anoints is Himself called God; "Thy throne O God, is for ever and ever." In this wonderful psalm, "The King" is both a man and God.

Isaiah calls the coming One a child born, and a Son given; His name is both, "The Mighty God" and "Prince of Peace" (Isa. 9:6).

Zechariah calls the coming One a shepherd. God Himself is the speaker in Zechariah 13:7, where He says, "Awake, O sword, against My shepherd, and against the man that is My fellow, saith the Lord of hosts: smite the shepherd, and the sheep shall be scattered." The smitten One is a man, and yet He is Jehovah's fellow.

This is the Jesus of prophecy; He is Christ the Lord. This is the Jesus of Paul's theology, and the Gospel's Jesus, too. This is Christ who is the Son of God, and who is Lord of all.

What a wonderful Person He is! The knowledge of His Deity enhances the grace of His lowliness. He did not "cry, nor lift up, nor cause His voice to be heard in the street" (Isa. 42:2). Our Lord was not a public agitator. He did not advertise His greatness. He never took advantage of popular acclaim. When they would have made Him a king, He withdrew into the wilderness and prayed.

Dr. Philip Schaff writes:

Heaven and earth seem to move around Him (Christ our Lord) as their center. What a contrast! A child in a manger, yet bearing the salvation of the world; a child hated and feared, yet longed for and loved; a child poor and despised, yet honored and adored—beset by danger yet marvelously preserved; a child setting the stars of heaven, the city of Jerusalem, the shepherds of Judea, and the sages of the East, in motion—attracting the best elements of the world, and repelling all that is dark and evil! This conception is too deep, too sublime, too significant, to be the invention of illiterate fishermen.

Both His person and His work, every word He spoke, and every act He performed, has the freshness, brilliance, and vigor of youth, and will retain it to the end of time. All other things fade away; every book of man loses its interest after repeated reading: but the gospel of Jesus never wearies; it becomes more interesting the more it is read, and grows deeper at every attempt to fathom its depth.

He was a humble individual, without friends and patrons in the Sanhedrin or at the court of Herod. He never mingled in familiar exchange with the religious or social leaders of the nation, whom He had startled in His twelfth year by His questions. He selected His disciples from among the illiterate fishermen of Galilee and promised them no reward in this world but a part in the bitter cup of His sufferings. He dined with publicans and sinners, and mingled with the common people, without ever condescending to their low manners and habits. He was so poor that He had no place to rest His head. He depended for the supply of His modest wants on the voluntary contributions of a few pious women; and the purse was in the hands of a thief and a traitor.

There never was in this world a life so unpretending, modest, and lowly in its outward form and condition, and yet producing such extraordinary effects upon all ages, nations, and classes of men.

Under His guidance a dozen poor, unlearned fishermen of Galilee, who without Him would have been buried in obscurity, have become the greatest teachers and benefactors of mankind! Where shall we look for a parallel case in history?

Jesus Christ is the most sacred, the most glorious, the most certain of all facts; arrayed in a beauty and majesty which throws the "starry heavens above us and the moral law within us" into obscurity, and fills us truly with ever growing reverence and awe. He shines forth with the self-evidencing light of the noonday sun. He is too great, too pure, too perfect, to have been invented by any sinful and erring man. His character and claims are confirmed by the sublimest doctrine, the purest ethics, the mightiest miracles, the grandest spiritual kingdom, and are daily and hourly exhibited in the virtues and graces of all who yield to the regenerating and sanctifying power of His spirit and example. The Lord Jesus Christ meets and satisfies all moral and religious aspirations.

The soul if left to its noblest impulses and aspirations, instinctively turns to Him, as the needle to the magnet, as the flower to the sun, as the panting hart to the fresh fountain. We are made for Him, and "our heart is without rest until it rests in Him." He commands our assent, He owns our affections and adoration. We cannot look upon Him without spiritual benefit. We cannot think of Him without being elevated above all that is low and mean, and encouraged to all that is good and noble. The very hem of His garment is healing to the touch. One hour spent in His communion outweighs all the pleasures of sin. He is the most precious gift of a merciful God to a fallen world. In Him are the treasures of wisdom; in Him the fountain of pardon and peace; in Him the only hope and comfort in this world and that which is to come...He is the glory of the past, the life of the present, and the hope of the future...According to an old Jewish proverb: "The secret of man is the secret of the Messiah." Christ is the great central Light of history, and, at the same time the Light of every soul: He alone can solve the mystery of our being, and fulfill the longings of our feelings after peace and happiness.

CHAPTER TWO

The Renown of His Birth

Our Lord Jesus Christ has renown for the manner of His coming into the world; He was renowned in His birth. Matthew, Luke, and John each tells his own story of this renown in the New Testament. One does not repeat what the other has told. There is a distinct purpose in each Evangelist's story of the coming of the Lord of Heaven to this earth of ours.

Matthew's story: Matthew first traces the royal genealogy down to "Jesus who is called Christ" from Abraham, through David, Solomon, and the kings. In this genealogy our Lord is seen coming to "confirm the promises made unto the fathers" (Rom. 15:8). Abraham had the "everlasting covenant" concerning the land of Canaan (Gen. 15:18), while David possessed the "everlasting covenant" concerning the kingdom and the throne (2 Sam. 7:16). In Matthew 1, our Lord has the renown of being born to be the promised King.

Luke's story: Luke first tells of His birth, then traces His human genealogy backward through Mary's father, through Nathan and David, to Adam, the head of the race. Luke tells all that needs to be known of the deep mystery of His being conceived of the Holy Ghost; and of His being born a Man and yet the Son of God (Lk. 1:30-35). In Luke our Lord has the renown of being born a Saviour into the world (Lk. 2:11).

John's story: John gives no details of His birth, and records no genealogy. John commences with sublime statements of the eternal deity of His person. John calls Him "The Word." In one brief statement the whole wonderful story is told, "The Word was made flesh and dwelt among us" (Jn. 1:14). In John our Lord's renown of being *God* is most emphatically revealed. All that the others tell of His birth, in John's Gospel is comprehended in the one word "made." "The Word was *made flesh,* and dwelt among us, and we beheld His glory, the glory as of the only begotten of the Father, full of grace and truth" (Jn. 1:14). These Gospel writers tell a three-part story in perfect harmony of the renown of our Lord and Saviour in His coming into the world.

In Matthew we have the genealogy of grace. The dark story of Judah's profligacy in Genesis 38, with its description of the dishonorable birth of Pharez, is written to show God's marvelous ways with men. It reveals also the ruin of the one who fathered the royal tribe. But for Matthew's genealogy, this dark page of Judah's history would never have been written.

By God's direction the royal descent was not through Judah's son Shelah, born in wedlock; but through Pharez, who though Judah's son, was an illigitimate child. Why did the line of royal descent, finding its way from Judah to David, run through so shameful a channel as it did, except to reveal the character of God's grace?

When Judah surrendered all the insignia of his tribal honor to the supposed harlot as a pledge, he had irretrievably lost all, but for God's sovereign grace. When the harlot could not be found, Judah said of the scepter, the bracelets, and the signet, "Let her take it to her, lest we be shamed" (Gen. 38:23). As far as Judah knew, the scepter was gone forever. And when Judah hypocritically thought that some other man was guilty, he said of his daughter-in-law, "Let her be burnt" (Gen. 38:24). When, however, the restored pledge condemned him, he replied, "She hath been more righteous than I" (Gen. 38:26).

It was the son of that unholy union—Pharez, through whom the scepter was preserved to Judah (Mt. 1:3). What triumphs of grace can be seen in these three names in Matthew's genealogy—Judah, Tamar and Pharez!

Count ten generations back from David, and you reach Pharez. Thus David was the tenth generation of an illigitimate son. In Deuteronomy 23:2 this word is found: "A bastard shall not enter into the congregation of the Lord: even to his tenth generation, shall he not enter into the congregation of the Lord."

This law would have excluded David the king, and all those in the royal line between him and Pharez.

The last five verses of the book of Ruth contain the names of ten men from Pharez to David. Is it not remarkable that that book of grace to a Gentile, Ruth of Moabitish blood, should end with ten generations of Pharez?

Why the generations of Pharez rather than the generations of Judah? It was only grace that brought into the congregation of the Lord any of those of the ten generations of a bastard; even David the king, for the tenth generation reached to him.

The next verse in Deuteronomy 23 places the same curse on a Moabite (see Deut. 23:3). This implies to a thinking soul that the same grace that brought into the congregation of the Lord ten generations of a bastard, can also bring in a woman of Moabitish blood. Ruth pleaded "grace" (Ruth 2:10), and Boaz the mighty man of wealth said, "I will redeem" (Ruth 4:1-12). The whole subject of Ruth 4 is "redemption." The insertion of the name Ruth in Matthew's genealogy (Mt. 1:5) brings to mind that lovely little book that bears her name.

Grace! Here again the genealogy runs down the channel of free grace. The whole story of Naomi, of apostasy and recovery, is introduced by that one name, "Ruth." Not only is the Gentile bride redeemed and purchased by Boaz; the fruit of that union— Obed, becomes to Naomi "the restorer of [her] life and the nourisher of [her] old age" (Ruth 4:15). The verse previous calls Obed Naomi's kinsman or redeemer. In this we have a picture of our Lord being a Redeemer to the remnant of Israel, after the redemption of the Bride is complete.

Before the names of Boaz and Ruth are reached, the genealogy contains the names of Salmon and Rachab (Mt. 1:5). Why does the inspired historian introduce the name of her that had been the harlot of Jericho? Did a prince of the house of Judah stoop so low as to lift up a woman of ill fame, and of Canaanite blood, and bring her into the royal line? Yes, Salmon did this. Was it to the tribe's dishonor? No, the very reverse. The fruit of that union was not a son of shame, but Boaz, the mighty man of wealth and power (Ruth 2:1). The same was true of another Prince of the tribe of Judah—Jesus Emmanuel; with whom Gentile sinners have been "quickened together" and with whom we have been "raised up together and made us sit together in heavenly places in Christ Jesus" (Eph. 2:5-6). This has been to "the praise of the glory of His grace" (Eph. 1:6).

What Salmon did in bringing Rahab into the congregation of the Lord was a sample and a type of our Mighty Prince's acts, who "raiseth up the poor from the dust, and lifteth up the beggar from the dunghill to set them among princes, and to make them inherit the throne of glory" (1 Sam. 2:8). Rahab of course was a changed woman when she was brought into the congregation of the Lord. (See Heb. 11:31.)

This is the channel of grace down which the royal line descends. There are repeated evidences everywhere of the utter ruin of man, but just as often the repeated introduction of the super-abounding grace of God.

This channel of God's grace in reaching Solomon, the builder of the temple, must run by way of the names of David, and of "her that had been the wife of Urias" (Mt. 1:6). The account does not say Bathsheba, lest you might forget David's great sin. The words, "...her that had been the wife of Urias," show that great transgression in all its dreadful memory.

Had grace not been sufficient to meet a very great sin in an highly honored person, the royal line never would have reached the name of Solomon. All the glory of Solomon and of his reign were the direct fruit of the irresistible grace of God.

Further down the line is the name of Jechonias, or Coniah (Mt. 1:11). God said of him, "As I live, saith the Lord, though Coniah, the son of Jehoiakim, king of Judah, were the signet upon my right hand, yet would I pluck thee thence" (Jer. 22:24). Yet of Zerubbabel, the grandson of Coniah, God says, "In that day, saith the Lord of Hosts, will I take thee, O Zerubbabel, my servant, the son of Shealtiel, saith the Lord, and will make thee as a signet: for I have chosen thee, saith the Lord of Hosts" (Hag. 2:23). This prophecy probably looks onward to that son of Zerubbabel—Joseph, the husband of Mary, who by taking Mary's child to be his legal son, handed the crown (or the title to it) down to Him.

Although our Lord of course was not begotten of Joseph, when he accepted Mary's unborn Son as his, Joseph became our Lord's legal father. When Joseph registered the name Jesus as his son at Bethlehem, the royal line from Solomon, Jechonias, and Joseph to Jesus was without a flaw.

In the virgin-born Son of Mary, Solomon had a son who was not his seed. The promise of Solomon's throne and kingdom being forever, was fulfilled. (See 2 Sam. 7:12; 1 Chron. 17:14; Ps. 89:36.)

Our Lord was as truly the heir of Joseph as Solomon was the heir of David. But all the conditional promises of God to Solomon, concerning his children and his house, were lost; for our Lord was not of Solomon's seed. For these conditional promises, see 1 Kings 2:4; 6:12; 8:25; 9:4-5; 1 Chronicles 28:9; and Psalm 132:12.

The double unconditional promise to David, concerning both his seed or house, and his throne or kingdom, is fulfilled through Nathan and through Solomon. (See 2 Sam. 7:12-16; 1 Chron. 17:10-14; Ps. 89:20-37; 1 Chron. 22:9-10.) The promises concerning David's throne descended through Solomon and Joseph to our Lord. The promises concerning David's seed and house, descended through Nathan and Mary (Lk. 3:31).

The explanation of Luke 3:23 is that Mary's father, Heli, had no sons, thus Joseph, his son-in-law, is called his son. Compare Numbers 36:1-13.

The curse on Coniah or Jechonias (Jer. 22:24-30) is fulfilled, for the Lord Jesus was not his seed, though through Joseph He was his legal son. The curse of Jeremiah 22 said of Jechonias, "No man of his seed shall prosper, sitting upon the throne of David, and ruling any more in Judah."

Had our Lord not been virgin born, this curse on Jechonias would have reached Him. There could be no man of the royal line of David, through Solomon and Jechonias, who could fulfill the promises to David and Solomon, but Christ. All others by natural generation would come under the curse of Jeremiah 22:29-30. This was pronounced by God's oath on all the seed of that wicked man. Joseph's son, begotten of him, could not be the king. He would have been the seed of Jechonias. But our Lord Jesus, born of a virgin, but in wedlock, was the legal son of Mary's husband; and so could inherit Jechonias' title, while completely escaping his curse.

Jechonias had the royal signet upon his hand all right. But

31

Jechonias was so wicked, that had he himself been the royal signet upon the hand of God, He would have plucked him thence. But Zerubbabel, of the seed of Jechonias, was made as a royal signet, for God in grace made choice of him (see Hag. 2:23). This looks on to Joseph, a true son of David, though descended from Zerubbabel and Jechonias, and on to Joseph's legal Son, Jesus. He receives the royal scepter, bracelets, and signet of Judah, through God's marvellous working as recorded in Matthew 1:18-25.

The curse of Jeremiah 22 stands; but so do the promises of 2 Samuel 7, and of 1 Chronicles 17, among others. By the virgin birth of our Lord, Solomon and Jechonias have a son who is not their seed; and by Him all the promises are Yea and Amen. "O the depth of the riches both of the wisdom and knowledge of God! How unsearchable are His judgments, and His ways past finding out" (Rom. 11:33).

The genealogy of Matthew is a testimony to the unity and to the inspiration of the Scriptures. It is a witness to the utter worthlessness of man. It bears eloquent testimony to the grace, wisdom, and power of God. That genealogy and the prophecies it connects with, demonstrate to a candid mind the necessity of the virgin birth and its accomplishment. "Thou shalt call His name Jesus: for He shall save His people from their sins" (Mt. 1:21). This word is like the fruit on a tree whose roots stretch into every part of the Old Testament Scriptures.

This first chapter of the New Testament supplies the sole reason for the writing of Genesis 38 and of the whole book of Ruth. The mourning and the music all point onward to His coming. The Kings and the Prophets unite in preparing for His coming. Our Lord Jesus Christ is the answer to the prophecies, and to the problems; all the lines converge on Him. He is the One, and there can be no other: God's words were fulfilled and Christ Jesus came.

We can see four reasons why our Lord Jesus Christ, the Son of God, was the legal son of Joseph the husband of Mary. They are:

1. Joseph did not make Mary a "public example," nor "put her away privily" when her condition became known to him. Read Matthew 1:19.

2. Joseph married Mary before her child was born, thereby

accepting her offspring as his own son.

3. Joseph acknowledged Jesus as his legal son when he called His name Jesus, and registered Him thus in the royal genealogy in Bethlehem. This was done without a word of explanation of any kind.

4. Joseph, until the day of his death, never disavowed these actions.

Down the line of the "generation" of Matthew's story, there are rather obscure but lovely characters, appearing now and again like stars in the firmament to brighten the moral darkness of the apostasy of the times. There are such men as Salmon, Boaz, and Zerubbabel; there are such women as Ruth, and Mary, the mother of our Lord. Yet no day was so dark as the day when Christ our Saviour was born. And no two characters shine with a holier, lovelier light than Joseph and Mary, the husband and wife to whom the care of God's precious Son was entrusted.

What a shock to Joseph's faithful love it must have been to discover what seemed like the indisputable evidence of Mary's unfaithfulness. What perplexity and sorrow Joseph's heart must have felt! As Joseph thought about what he should do, the true nobility of his loving and gracious spirit comes out. He was not even "willing" to make her a public example. That would have cleared his own name from reproach, but Joseph's tender love was still so deep for Mary that he could not endure to think of the suffering this would cause her. Joseph would sooner have shame upon himself, just man though he was, than to have one he loved, though guilty, suffer the consequences of her supposed wrongdoing. "Joseph was minded to put her away privily." In that case, many would have supposed that after his lack of moral restraint, he had lost his interest in his espoused wife. What a noble spirit that was to suffer himself, rather than to let the seemingly guilty one bear the shame of wrongdoing!

Joseph was poor, extremely poor. Instead of David's royal city Bethlehem, he was living in the dirty little village of Nazareth. Instead of being a mighty man of wealth like Boaz, Joseph was a common carpenter. But Joseph was rich, rich in the treasures of the kingdom of God; rich with that rare treasure of the spirit of grace. When at last Joseph knew the blessed truth of Mary's coming Son, and of His conception of the Holy Ghost, what shame he and Mary did bear together, even the reproach of Christ in His birth!

Mary also—what wonderful fortitude and trust in the living God she manifested; telling Joseph nothing till God interposed on her behalf. How Mary's heart must have pained as she watched the face of Joseph, who was to her the dearest one on earth! How strong that patient spirit that could wait for God so long! Mary left herself entirely in the hands of God. What noble faith that was! That was the spirit that expressed itself in that lovely song of praise, "My soul doth magnify the Lord. And my spirit hath rejoiced in God my Saviour. For He hath regarded the low estate of His handmaiden: for, behold, from henceforth all generations shall call me blessed. For He that is mighty hath done to me great things; and holy is His name" (Lk. 1:46-55).

"Behold the days come, saith the Lord, that I will raise unto David a righteous *Branch*; and a King shall reign and prosper, and shall execute judgment and justice in the earth. In His days Judah shall be saved, and Israel shall dwell safely: and this is His name whereby He shall be called, *The Lord Our Righteousness*" (Jer. 23:5-6).

Here was "the *Branch* that Thou madest strong for Thyself" (Ps. 80:15). Or as verse 17 of the same psalm declares: "Let Thy hand be upon the Man of Thy right hand, upon the Son of Man whom Thou madest strong for Thyself."

This is the Branch, the Plant that comes out of the "stem" or stump of Jesse. "There shall come forth a rod out of the stem of Jesse, and a Branch shall grow out of His roots" (Isa. 11:1). Jesse's family was a ruined house. The tree was long since cut down; only the stump and roots remained. Everything was as hopeless as could be. There is a remarkable verse about a tree in the book of Job, that could refer to this family tree of Jesse and David. "For there is hope of a tree, if it be cut down, that it will sprout again, and that the tender branch thereof will not cease. Though the root thereof wax old in the earth, and the stock (stump) thereof die in the ground; yet through the scent of water it will bud, and bring forth boughs like a plant" (Job 14:7-9).

David's whole inheritance for five centuries had been like this tree cut down with only its dead stump in the ground, when our Lord came to the world. Though all seemed so absolutely hopeless, yet out of that dead stump, and out of those roots in the ground, a living Branch came forth. That Branch was the Son of Man. That living sprout was the Lord Jesus.

This coming of a Living Branch from a dead stump was a practical resurrection. The coming of the Plant of Renown from Matthew's ruined genealogy was a being "raised up." Zacharias made mention of this when he said, "The Lord God of Israel... hath *raised up* an horn of salvation for us in the house of His servant David" (Lk. 1:69).

What did Abraham or David possess in the days of Herod the king? No more than the Plantagenets of four hundred years ago possess in England today. Everything was lost centuries before. That is, everything tangible and real in the eyes of men. Abraham's children did not own the land, and David's sons did not possess the kingdom. Then why call Jesus Christ the son of David, the son of Abraham? Neither of these fathers had any inheritance to be possessed by their sons now. There was one thing that yet remained; it was the root of the tree in the ground. There was one thing that these fathers still possessed and that was the Word of God.

The people, the land, the city, and the throne were all lost; but the promises of God remained. Matthew's first chapter tells the story, how the last King of the line of Solomon was "raised up" by God. It was life from the dead. It was the clean out of the unclean. It was a Living Branch from a dead stump. "The birth of Jesus Christ was on this wise." Those words never needed to be said of any birth from Seth to Him. By the Holy Spirit the chasm was bridged. Joseph had a Son who was begotten of God, and whom God names Jesus Emmanuel. The seed of the royal family was vitiated and cursed forever in Jechonias. Only God and His promise remained. Virgin birth was the only possible way to escape the curse and death.

In the most simple, artless way possible, the words of Matthew's first chapter tell how it was accomplished. "Now all this was done, that it might be fulfilled which was spoken of the Lord by the prophet, saying, Behold, a virgin shall be with child, and shall bring forth a son, and they shall call His name Emmanuel, which being interpreted is, God with us" (Mt. 1:22-23). This is the story of how our Lord "was made of the seed of

David according to the flesh" (Rom. 1:3); how the Branch, the King, was brought forth by the God of resurrection to fulfill every promise to Abraham and David concerning the land and the kingdom.

It is a marvelous story of God's perfect weaving of the acts of His grace into the broken and otherwise ruined history of men. "Thou shalt call His name Jesus: for He shall save His people from their sins" (Mt. 1:21). Sins! Sins! This was the ruin. Jesus! Jesus! He was the remedy. Praise God forever!

CHAPTER THREE

Words Like No Other

"Never man spake like this man" (Jn. 7:46).

These words were spoken by officers of Jerusalem who were sent by the chief priests and Pharisees to arrest the Lord and bring Him before them. This was their only excuse for having failed in their duty, and for returning without their prisoner. When those officers left the Sanhedrin, they were filled with blind prejudice against Christ. It seemed to them that all the holiest and the greatest men of the city took Jesus of Nazareth for a deceiver and a malefactor. Among the Pharisees He was listed as a blasphemer; He was called a Samaritan; He was accused of casting out demons through Beelzebub, the prince of demons. There was no name too vile to give to Christ; there was no motive too base to ascribe to Him. This was the atmosphere in which these officers lived. These were the opinions they heard expressed about Jesus Christ day after day. The position of leadership the priests occupied, and the reputation for holiness and truth they possessed, made it practically impossible that these uninstructed officers should think anything different of Him. The prejudiced minds of these commissioned servants of the temple caused them to feel they were going to arrest one who was guilty of scattering blasphemies among the people.

Why were these temple officers so powerless to take our Lord? What so completely changed their attitude that they dared return to those who sent them without the Man they were sent to arrest? How could they brave the scorn of the chief

priests and Pharisees? What excuse did they have to give? It was
the words of the Lord Jesus that had wrought the change; their
only excuse was: "Never man spake like this man."

All the words those officers heard numbered (in English) thirty-one. Just thirty-one words and each of them a word so simple
that a child could understand it. "If any man thirst, let him come
unto Me, and drink. He that believeth on Me, as the Scripture
hath said, out of his belly shall flow rivers of living water" (Jn.
7:37-38).

These were the words the officers heard fall from His lips as
He stood and cried among the crowded streets of Jerusalem during the Feast of Tabernacles. Why did they say, "Never man
spake like this man"?

There are three reasons at least why these words of Christ are
different from the words of any other man. They are: (i) because
of the words themselves; (ii) because of the way He said them;
and (iii) because of the effect of these words on those that heard
them.

"If any man thirst...." Souls of men have been thirsty ever
since Adam turned his back on God. Thirsty for rest; thirsty for
peace; thirsty for eternal life; thirsty for God. The greatest and
the least; the wisest and the most simple; the outcast and the
Pharisee, they all know this thirst. Here was a Man who dared
to cry, "If any man thirst, let him come unto Me and drink." If
He were only a man, these words were among the most blasphemous ever spoken. Had any other man but Christ said these
words, he would be either pitied as a madman, or scorned as a
most notorious blasphemer. No one feels that way about Him.
These words from His lips carry with them the simple conviction of truth, so that without the least effort we bow our hearts
to their blessed proclamation. But what wonderful words they
are! Think of Him being able to quench the thirst of anyone anywhere! This stranger from Galilee! This "carpenter" from
Nazareth declaring He could meet the deep desires of the souls
of men. How utterly stupendous the declaration! How absolutely God-like the promises! Surely, never man spake like this Man.

The glory of the Gospelers of the New Testament is that they
don't speak of themselves. Matthew mentions his own name
only when absolutely necessary: "Matthew, the publican" (Mt.

10:3). Mark never mentions himself at all. Mark wrote the life of Christ as an eyewitness, evidently; he served the church of God for at least thirty years and was a co-laborer of the foremost of the apostles; yet not a word of John Mark is found anywhere in the New Testament.

The same is true of Luke, "the beloved physician," who wrote both the Gospel that bears his name and the Book of Acts. Except for the prologue, where he addressed his friend, "the most excellent Theophilus," Luke makes no reference to himself whatever. But for the change of the pronouns "they" and "we," one could not tell when Luke the historian was a member of the little band. These writers obliterated their own personality from their writings.

John also, who wrote the fourth Gospel, speaks most stintingly of himself, as "the disciple whom Jesus loved" or "that other disciple." The absolute hiding of the writers in these imperishable stories of Christ is without a parallel in human literature. The glory of the four Evangelists is their absolute silence about themselves.

But the glory of the Lord Jesus is in the wonderful things He says about Himself, and about His words. It has been said that, "self-consciousness is the disease of the soul." This is true of any ordinary man; but it was not true of Christ. Another has written, "To say such things of oneself as come from His lips is a sign of a weak, foolish nature. It is fatal to all influence, to all beauty of character. He declares Himself possessed of virtues which, if a man said he had them, it would be the best proof that he did not possess them and did not know himself."

Here is a sampling of the Lord's statements concerning Himself: "I am the way, the truth, and the life"; "I am the light of the world"; a "greater than Jonas is here," a "greater than Solomon," a "greater than the temple," and then having said these things, He declares, "I am meek and lowly of heart." And multitudes believe Him, and say, "Yes! it is true." How accurate the words of the officers of the temple, "Never man spake like this man."

It took Jacob all his life to learn the meaning of the name "God Almighty." God was to Abraham, Isaac and Jacob the All-Sufficient One. To Moses, the Lord revealed the meaning of the exalted name, Jehovah. David and Solomon spoke many inspired words of the God they knew and trusted. They were all servants, but Jesus was God's Son, and in the most familiar way repeatedly said, "My Father." When He was risen from the dead, He said to Mary Magdalene, "I ascend unto My Father, and your Father; and to My God, and your God" (Jn. 20:17). What marvelous words these are! "As the Father knoweth Me, even so know I the Father: and I lay down My life for the sheep" (Jn. 10:15), He said. "For the Father loveth the Son, and showeth Him all things that Himself doeth...For as the Father raiseth up the dead, and quickeneth them; even so the Son quickeneth whom He will. For the Father judgeth no man, but hath committed all judgment unto the Son. That all men should honor the Son, even as they honor the Father. He that honoreth not the Son honoreth not the Father which hath sent Him" (Jn. 5:20-23).

Who but the eternal Son could say, "He that hath seen Me hath seen the Father" (Jn. 14:9) or, "All things that the Father hath are Mine" (Jn. 16:15) or, "I and My Father are one" (Jn. 10:30)? And hear Him pray, "Father, I will that they also, whom Thou hast given Me, be with Me where I am; that they may behold My glory which Thou hast given Me; for Thou lovest Me before the foundation of the world" (Jn. 17:24).

We who have listened to these precious words from His lips concerning the Father, can surely say, "Never man spake like this man."

Listen to His own testimony to the words He spoke: "The words that I speak unto you, they are spirit, and they are life" (Jn. 6:63). "Verily, Verily, I say unto you, He that heareth My word, and believeth on Him that sent Me, hath everlasting life, and shall not come into condemnation; but is passed from death unto life" (Jn. 5:24). "He that rejecteth Me, and receiveth not My words, hath one that judgeth him: the word that I have spoken, the same shall judge him in the last day" (Jn. 12:48). "If a man love Me he will keep My words: and My Father will love him, and We will come unto him, and make Our abode with him" (Jn. 14:23). "If ye abide in Me and My words abide in you, ye shall ask what ye will, and it shall be done unto you" (Jn. 15:7).

Infidels and Unitarians confess the words of Christ to be true, and yet deny His deity. You would wonder if they ever read what He said. Theodore Parker did not believe in the deity of Christ, and did his best to destroy the faith of others. He wrote of the Lord Jesus: "Christ unites in Himself the sublimest precepts, and the divinest practices—rises free from all the prejudices of his age—pours out a doctrine beautiful as the light, sublime as heaven and as true as God." All we would say to Mr. Parker is this, If the doctrine of Christ be beautiful as the light, *He is the Light;* if the doctrine of Christ be as true as God, *He is God.* Could Christ be true and His words false? Christ Himself is The Truth; and His words are like Himself.

Notice that His words were not written by Himself. As far as we can gather, there was no writing of the words of the Lord Jesus during His lifetime, except in the hearts of His hearers. "Mary kept all these things, and pondered them in her heart" (Lk. 2:19). "And they remembered His words" (Lk. 24:8). The only writing of our Lord was with His finger, and that in the loose sand of the ground (Jn. 8:6).

Other men who spoke words acclaimed by their fellows wrote in books to preserve to themselves a perpetual memorial of literary glory. Not so the Son of God. When He expired, forsaken on the cross, His words only remained sown on the hearts of men. There the Holy Spirit, like the sun and the rain, made them bear fruit after His resurrection.

When the Lord Jesus died, His works were doubted; His disciples seemed hopeless, and His words appeared lost, like the seed of the harvest, in the cold ground during the frozen winter. Peter had said, "Thou hast the words of eternal life," but those words were not written, and now Peter has denied Him in the presence of His enemies. The officers testified, "Never man spake like this man," but now they have seen Him answering not a word, "like a lamb dumb before her shearers, so He opened not His mouth." All His friends were disappointed, and despaired when He was crucified. Who now would care about His words? The tree is cut down; how can it now bear any fruit? No other person's words have been so cherished as the words of the Lord Jesus; no other person's words would be remembered at all, were they not written when he was living.

Imperishable words! Here then is one of the wonders of the words of Christ. His words are indestructible. He said, "Heaven

41

and earth shall pass away, but My words shall not pass away" (Mt. 24:35). Millions of people lived when He lived. Countless millions had lived and died before Him. How very few of them spoke words that have survived the centuries! Thousands enjoyed the advantages of learning and culture; but of Him they said, "How knoweth this man letters, having never learned?" (Jn. 7:15).

Except for Christ, the words of Pilate and of Caiaphas, would have passed away; drowned in the oblivion of a forgotten generation. Greece was then a nation of scholars, but how few of her favored sons were able, by their riches and their genius, to preserve and pass on their wisdom and their words to coming generations. They had the advantage of embalming words in books and libraries of a cultured people; and yet the words of the chosen few wise men of earth during our Lord's day have perished. They lie entombed on dusty shelves in unread books of ancient languages; but the words of Him whom they called "the carpenter," live still. His words have not passed away.

There was no feverish haste to write His words, or to have them written, when the tide was turning against Him, and He knew His hour had come. As the husbandman sows his seed, by the wayside, on stony ground, on thorny as well as on good ground, so had He sown His words. Well He knew what the result would be: "The words that I speak unto you, they are spirit and they are life."

How unlikely it seemed! Judea was a small, obscure country. The Jews were not a renowned people. Nazareth had a dishonorable reputation even in its own district. It was Nathanael, a Galilean, who asked, "Can any good thing come out of Nazareth?" Joseph and Mary were so poor that they had to take advantage of the provision of the law in the case of extreme poverty, "two turtle doves or two young pigeons" (Lev. 12:8). Jesus of Nazareth was a carpenter; His disciples were poor fishermen; He sought and found no patronage from priests or kings; He could hardly number among His chosen disciples one rich or influential person; His name was unknown in the schools and colleges of the land; He was despised and rejected of men; and yet He said, "Heaven and earth shall pass away, but My words shall not pass away" (Mt. 24:35).

Could the whole world have heard, the whole world would have laughed in ridicule and scorn at the impossibility of such a thing. But those words were true. Unlike the words of mortal men that turn to ashes like themselves, the words of Christ are enduring and eternal. His words did not have to be preserved by the art of publication, so that being shelved among the monuments of the past, they would continue. His words are living words; they grow like the seed in the hearts of His people, and shall bloom and bear fruit through time and eternity. They have not passed away, nor shall they.

To compound the issue, His words were distasteful to men. Listen to the testimony of the Scriptures: "This is an hard saying; who can hear it?...Many of His disciples went back, and walked no more with Him" (Jn. 6:60, 66). "Not that which goeth into the mouth defileth a man; but that which cometh out of the mouth, this defileth a man. Then came His disciples, and said unto Him, Knowest Thou that the Pharisees were offended, after they heard this saying?" (Mt. 15:11-12). "There was a division therefore among the Jews for these sayings. And many of them said, He hath a devil, and is mad: why hear ye Him?" (Jn. 10:19-20).

The words of the Lord Jesus make nothing of man or his works. Ahab said of Michaiah, "I hate him: for he doth not prophesy good concerning me, but evil" (1 Ki. 22:8). For this reason, our Lord was hated also. He called the Pharisees hypocrites, and continually raised their ire, especially when they discovered that His parables were spoken against them (Mk. 12:12). The leaders of the nation of Israel hated His words more than His works: when the common people heard Him gladly, they said, "He deceiveth the people" (Jn. 7:12). When the blind man in his simplicity said, "He is a prophet" (Jn. 9:17), the Jews said to Christ, "Thou art a Samaritan and hast a devil" (Jn. 8:48). "And there was a division among them" (Jn. 9:16).

Yet His words lived! Here, then, is a wonder in the words of Christ; they were imperishable words. The men of letters and of power condemned His words, and rejected His sayings, and yet those words lived. Those who alone seemed able to collect and record the words of Jesus Christ and to give them honorable sanction by their approbation were all implacable enemies to His sayings, refusing them with bitterest scorn and derision; and yet those words lived.

No college gathered His words to deposit them with its treasures of literature. No Gamaliel or Josephus sent abroad the words of the prophet of Nazareth, with the advantage of his endorsement. The wise and the devout both repudiated with all the sarcasm or violence of their natures, the words of truth, meekness, and righteousness which were spoken at the temple in Jerusalem, or in the villages of Galilee. "Are we blind also?" asked the self-satisfied, but empty religionists. The words of the Lord Jesus had cut them deeply. "We be Abraham's seed, and were never in bondage to any man" (Jn. 8:33). He answered, "He that committeth sin is the servant of sin." Said they, "We be not born of fornication; we have one Father, even God." He answered, "Ye are of your father the devil." Before the interview ended, they took up stones to stone Him because of His words. (See Jn. 8:31-59.) But all His enemies could not crush His words. The seed was sown and would grow in spite of anger and opposition. Priests and Pharisees hated and banned the words of Christ, but those words lived on. Heaven with its glory, and earth with its riches might pass away; but His words would not pass away.

The attitude of men of lifeless religion and men of letters toward the words of the Lord Jesus has never changed. The "church" which should have fed the world with the "bread of God" has hidden the corrupting leaven in the "three measures of meal" till it all was leavened. Little by little, slowly but surely, that growing system that called itself the church of Christ took away the words of the Lord from the people. Ultimately Babylon obtained universal and absolute authority in the nations of the earth. That power, with the infliction of death in its most painful forms was used against the perpetuation and knowledge of the words of Christ. The deep and sinister purpose of that system that named His name, was to effectively destroy His life-giving words forever from among men.

Plowmen and tradesmen, as well as elders and preachers were imprisoned and burned for reading and repeating the precious life-giving words of the Lord Jesus. Blind and superstitious clergy of an intolerant, world-domineering system were determined to destroy utterly by fire and sword all knowledge of the words of Christ—and those who cherished them.

Fifteen centuries passed since the battle was commenced by the scribes and Pharisees; it had raged continuously through the years of ignorance and spiritual darkness that intervened; and now it seemed that the powers of hell would crush with violence the light from among men. But no, every Pharaoh lifted up his hand in vain. Every Annas and Caiaphas looked dismayed upon the crushing of their hopes. The word of the Lord grew and multiplied. All the powers of fire and hell could not suppress His sayings who uttered these words, "Heaven and earth shall pass away but my word shall not pass away." The Bible was translated at great cost into the languages of the people, printed and distributed widely during the Reformation.

Bibles are more plentiful today than they ever have been. The words of the Lord Jesus are better known and loved by a greater multitude today than ever before in the history of the world. The Gospels have been handed down by the noblest of earth, through rivers of blood, at the cost of liberty and life, in the history of every nation in Christendom. Christians have fought by weakness, enemies as diverse as Herod, Pontius Pilate, and the people of Israel, and have always been victorious. The enemy, the devil, in one age, has prepared his weapons in the monasteries of superstition; in another he has conducted his warfare from the colleges of infidelity; but whether Greek or Jew, ignorant or intellectual, every weapon has failed.

Passed away! What has passed away? The kings of earth have passed away. The cruelty of the Inquisition and the scoffings of Voltaire have passed away. Whatever opposition may arise to God and His Word shall surely pass away: for the Son of Man who was Son of God, said, "Heaven and earth shall pass away, but My word shall not pass away."

Let the ages answer. Let history come with the officers to the seat of power and learning. With one voice all will say, "Never man spake like this Man."

The words of the Lord Jesus were often promises as well as declarations. They were promises that could be tested; promises that *have* been tested, thousands and thousands of times. Whoever found fault with Matthew 11:28? Was there ever a man or woman who protested that these words should be declared a libel, "Come unto Me, all ye that labor and are heavy laden, and I will give you rest"?

Princess Elizabeth was found dead in her prison, with her head resting on these precious words in her open Bible. Queen Victoria of Britain has the whole depicted in a monument of stone, where the gracious; maiden died. Under the stone the words of Jesus of Nazareth are inscribed, "Come unto Me…I will give you rest." Has any British atheist ever suggested the monument should be destroyed because of the libel it advertises? Not that I ever heard.

Augustine said, "I have read many wonderful and beautiful words in Plato and Cicero, but I never read there, "Come unto Me, all ye that labor and are heavy laden, and I will give you rest."

The words of the Lord Jesus were like the heavens that declare the glory of God, and like the firmament that shows His handiwork. They are like the stars that shine forever.

We get so used to the stars being there that we seldom look at them, and completely forget their glory. When some of Napoleon's generals were contending there was no God, the Emperor led them outside the tent and pointed to the stars, "If there be no God," said Napoleon, "who made all these?"

In the same spirit we would point to the words of Jesus the Christ, and say to those who doubt the truth of the gospel story, "Who spoke all these?" The miracles of Christ are not more wonderful than His words.

There is a fly in the ointment of the words of the best of men. Moses spoke unadvisedly with his lips (Ps. 106:33); Peter was guilty of dissimulation, and Paul had to rebuke him (Gal. 2:13). Paul himself had to retract what he said in the courtroom (Acts 23:5). Job, the patient one, opened his mouth and cursed his day (Job 3:1). Elijah uttered words of discouragement and had to be reproved (1 Ki. 19:9-10). But Jesus of Nazareth never uttered a word that revealed any of the frailties and faults of the whole human race. Like the Passover lamb, His words were "without blemish"; and like the Bride's description of Him, "altogether lovely."

What little follies in the writings and in the words of the holiest of men! But every word of our Lord Jesus Christ was like the most fine gold; or like the frankincense that even when "beaten small," emitted its lovely fragrance from every particle. How could this be if He were but a mere man? Surely "Never man spake like this man."

Our Lord, living in an eternal calm, never hesitated in the face of infinite difficulty. He did not fear to say to the raging elements, "Peace! Be still!" (Mk. 4:39).

Canute, the Danish king of England, moved his throne near the waves of the incoming tide. His admirers told him the waves would obey his word. Canute's submission to their desires caused them all shame; for had he not moved himself and his throne back again, all would have been overthrown by the sea. Proud words from men carry the refutation of their own emptiness and worthlessness.

Our Lord did not hesitate to cry aloud, so all could hear, "Lazarus, come forth!"; nor to say in the house of Gentiles weeping, "Maid, arise!" There was calm and yet majestic power in His words when the greatest issues were at stake. His words healed the leper, and liberated the enslaved demoniac. His utterances never failed.

All creation bowed as a slave at His feet. The winds and the sea obeyed Him. The unbroken colt submitted to His commands. The fig tree withered at a word from Him. There was not a sphere where His word did not prevail with irresistible power. The disciples were astonished when the storm ceased, and said, "What manner of man is this?" It was His word of power that baffled them; they said, "Even the wind and the sea obey Him" (Mk. 4:41).

Today there is such a deluge of words written to be read that if the citizens of any American community had to read all that the papers printed, they would have time for nothing else. All the minutes of all the hours would not suffice to devour a tenth of this refuse that is being dumped in the language of the American people. Words pour out daily like water when a dam gives way. This is the generation of words. Words over the air the people cannot listen to; words in the newspapers that the people cannot read. These words are like the insects of the summer time; or the passing bloom on the flowers of the field; they die as soon as they live. Hero lovers use all the arts of their train-

47

ing to embalm the words of their admired heroes; but a year or two suffices to leave these words buried in the oblivion of a forgotten past.

A scorning infidel wrote of the words of Christ: "The words of Jesus are less than the words of the Lindbergh-Morrow wedding in one issue of one newspaper!" Is that scorn, or is it glory? Who should laugh, the Christian or the infidel? Who cares today what was written in the newspapers concerning the Lindbergh wedding? Those words, like the words of the infidel, have lost their interest long ago. But not the words of Christ. His words are still "More to be desired than gold; yea, than much fine gold; sweeter also than honey and the honeycomb" (Ps. 19:10).

When many disciples left the Lord and went away because, as they said, "This is an hard saying; who can hear it?" (Jn. 6:60), our Lord turned to the twelve and said, "Will ye also go away?" Impetuous Peter immediately expressed the devotion of his, and of their hearts, in the words, "Lord, to whom shall we go? Thou hast *the words of eternal life*" (Jn. 6:68).

Did any philosopher or sage ever speak words of eternal life? Did you ever stop to consider the wonder of the words in John 3:16? "For God so loved the world, that He gave His only begotten Son; that whosoever believeth in Him, should not perish, but have everlasting life."

These words have been translated into most of the spoken languages of men. What no sage of Africa ever knew; what no heart in Asia ever conceived; Christ has spoken. But for these words of eternal life, the Queen of Sheba might still sit in darkness on her throne, and the land of Ethiopia stretch out her hands to God in vain.

All the writings of oriental philosophy are wanderings in the darkness; they contain no words of "eternal life." Socrates and Confucius could not look beyond the stars. It was not philosophy that revealed these precious words to us. They come from the very heart of God and are made known through the lips of His Son. None of the gods of the heathen is represented as loving men. Such knowledge was too wonderful for blinded fools that crawled upon the earth. There has been but One on this earth who could say, "He that heareth My word, and believeth on Him that sent Me hath everlasting life."

48

Not surprisingly, heaven's words come only from heaven. You could get the fragrance of roses from a dungeon, if first the lovely flowers were carried there. This fragrant knowledge of a God of love could never have been told except by the lips of the One who came from His Father in heaven. He alone could speak words of eternal life.

In almost every chapter of John's inspiring Gospel, these words of eternal life are found. A learned rabbi hears them at night from an object lesson of Moses lifting up the serpent in the wilderness (3:14). An ignorant and licentious, though religious Samaritan woman hears them from "a prophet" who sits on Sychar's well (4:14). A hopeless paralytic, waiting thirty-eight years at Bethesda's pool, hears them also, and so did those that day who accused the Mighty Healer of making a man whole on the Sabbath day. "Verily, verily, I say unto you: He that heareth My word, and believeth on Him that sent Me, hath everlasting life; and shall not come into condemnation, but is passed from death unto life" (5:24). There were words of eternal life when He fed the hungry multitudes with five loaves and two small fishes, "I am the Bread of Life: he that cometh to Me shall never hunger; and he that believeth on Me shall never thirst" (6:35).

Hear His words about the living water when the unsatisfied crowd at Jerusalem kept the feast of Tabernacles: "If any man thirst, let him come unto Me, and drink. He that believeth on Me, as the Scripture hath said, out of his belly shall flow rivers of living water" (7:37). Read words about eternal life when He opened the eyes of the blind in chapter 9, words about Himself as the resurrection and the life, when He wept with others at the grave of Lazarus.

These words of eternal life took deep root in the hearts of His disciples, and when the cross blasted their superficial expectations, His resurrection raised them again to a living hope, for they remembered His words.

All the utterances of the Lord Jesus were full of wisdom and grace. How beautifully perfect were His first recorded words as He sat among the doctors at Jerusalem! "How is it that ye sought Me? know ye not that I must be about My Father's business?" (Lk. 2:49). What a gentle rebuke to His mother, who had said, "Thy father and I have sought thee sorrowing." The absolute commonplace of His life at Nazareth had evidently clouded in Mary's memory the truth of His Sonship of God. It is written there, "His mother kept all these sayings in her heart" (Lk. 2:51).

When the Pharisees thought they had Him in a trap, whichever way He answered their question, "Is it lawful to give tribute to Caesar or not?" (Mt. 22:17), how utterly they were silenced by the perfection of His answer! "Render therefore unto Caesar the things which are Caesar's; and unto God the things that are God's" (Mt. 22:21).

The perfect wisdom of the Lord shines out again when He answered the question of the priests of the temple by asking them another. Their question was, "By what authority doest Thou these things, and who gave Thee this authority?" He answered, "I also will ask you one thing, which if ye tell Me, I in like wise will tell you by what authority I do these things. The baptism of John, whence was it? from heaven, or of men?" (Mt. 21:23-25). Had it fitted their case, they would have said either. They dared not to say, "Of men," for they feared the people who all took John for a prophet; they would not say, "Of God," for that would have authenticated both Him and His mission. So they said, "We cannot tell." He justly answered, "Neither tell I you by what authority I do these things." The reference to the baptism of John answered their question as to His authority, had they the honesty to face it.

The bitterest opposition of the Pharisees was to the fact of our Lord being the Son of God. "While the Pharisees were gathered together, Jesus asked them, saying, What think ye of Christ? Whose son is He? They say unto Him, The son of David. He saith unto them, How then doth David in spirit call him Lord, saying, The Lord said unto my Lord, Sit thou on my right hand, till I make thine enemies thy footstool? If David call him Lord, how is He his son?" (Mt. 22:41-45). The record ends with these words, "And no man was able to answer Him a word, neither dared any man from that day forth ask Him any more questions" (Mt. 22:46). For this question of the Lord Jesus involved either denying the inspiration of David's writing in the Psalms, or else the acknowledgment that Messiah was the Son of God.

The wisdom and understanding of our Lord was clearer than

the noonday. His answers were "clear as the sun, fair as the moon, and terrible as an army with banners." It was the perfection of His wise and searching words that caused Peter to say, "Lord, Thou knowest all things; Thou knowest that I love Thee" (Jn. 21:17).

Job desired that his words might be written with an iron pen, and with lead in the rock forever (see Job 19:23-24). But monuments of stone will wear away and their inscriptions perish. The words of Christ spoken in Judea and Galilee, and written in the Scriptures, are not only remembered on earth, they are forever settled in heaven. There the beauty of those precious words will never wear away.

They had a way of preserving fruit a hundred years ago that I understand is now lost. I have seen a dish of oranges and apples that looked as lovely as though freshly plucked from the trees. That fruit was seventy-five years old. It looked nice but it was as hard as rock. It was only good to look at; it could not be eaten. This is like the preserved words of ancient men; the volumes look nice on library shelves, but not one in a hundred would take the trouble to read them, or to listen to them being read. Their power and life are gone.

The ancient writings are mostly heavy, dead, and uninteresting; but the souls of men still feed on the words of Christ today as they did a thousand years ago. "The words that I speak unto you, they are spirit and they are life" (Jn. 6:63). In this His words are different; they are fresh and satisfying, like fruit from our orchards in the summertime. Truly, "Never man spake like this Man."

When the son of Count de las Cases read the Sermon on the Mount to Napoleon and other notables in St. Helena, the emperor expressed himself "struck with the highest admiration of the purity, the sublimity, the beauty of the morality which it contained." The Count confessed, "We all experienced the same feeling."

In a Roman Catholic country a colporteur called at a house to offer Bibles for sale. The ignorant people only knew what their spiritual advisors had told them of the Book. "Bible!" said a young woman, "why that is a bad book and the devil wrote it." "Let us see," replied the undaunted colporteur, "we will read a portion and you shall judge who wrote it." He turned to John's Gospel, and read part of the fourteenth chapter ending with: "Peace I leave with you, My peace give I unto you; not as the world giveth, give I unto you; let not your heart be troubled, neither let it be afraid." He waited. There were tears in the maiden's eyes. "Who wrote it?" said he. With the utmost assurance the answer came, "That book has come from heaven; those words are the words of God."

Why does mighty unbelief and darkest superstition bow in homage before the words of Jesus of Nazareth, acknowledging the power and grace of these searching, yet comforting messages? Why does atheism hush its scornings and opposition, drop its sword when Jesus speaks? It is because *His words are the words of God.* Peter long ago breathed the sentiment of all true Christians when he said of Christ, "Lord, to whom shall we go? Thou hast the words of eternal life; and we believe, and are sure, that Thou *art* the Christ, the Son of the living God." What an impossible position—to place the crown of glory and honor upon His words, and the crown of thorns upon His person!

No one perhaps ever wrote so blasphemous a book and called it *"The Life of Jesus"* as Renan. Philip Schaff calls Renan a great Orientalist and remarks, "We can hardly trust our eyes when we see Renan digging from the grave of disgrace and contempt the exploded hypothesis of vulgar imposture." But even Renan confesses in his book, "The hero of Nazareth is without an equal," and "his glory remains perfect and will be renewed forever." So God allows the bitterest enemies of His Christ to prophesy their own undoing and eternal shame in writing words of triumphant and eternal glory, concerning the words of the Son of God. The greatest enemies of the gospel in every age have borne testimony to the truth of the officers' words, "Never man spake like this Man." How much more honest and honorable to bow like Peter at His feet, drinking His words of eternal life into our hearts and confessing with our mouth, "We believe and are sure that Thou art the Christ the Son of the living God."

Rummaging amid the refuse in a temple in inaccessible Tibet, a Buddhist priest picked up a torn piece of paper. That paper contained words of the Lord Jesus Christ. This man did not know who had written or spoken these words. His heart asked no question of the truth or authority of the message, but in response to them, he put on sackcloth, and was broken in repentance immediately, for he felt that God had spoken. All the Buddhist priest read was, "Blessed are the pure in heart for they shall see God." This poor devotee of a hopeless religion cried, "I am not pure in heart; I shall not see God." This one arrow slew all his spiritual pride. One sentence from the lips of Jesus our Lord turned a bigoted Buddhist into a conscience-stricken sinner. The wound that the words made was later healed by the balm of the gospel. "Come unto Me, all ye that labor, and are heavy laden, and I will give you rest." The Buddhist priest heard, came, and was saved.

Whether in Tibet or America, among sages or among savages, the words of the Lord Jesus have had the same effect and wrought the same results. A multitude which no man can number shall one day bow at His feet who redeemed them by His blood and who comforted them with His words. And they will say, "Thou art worthy...for Thou wast slain, and hast redeemed us unto God by Thy blood" (Rev. 5:9).

While Abraham, the chief of the patriarchs, said, "I am but dust and ashes"; and Isaiah, the chief of prophets, said, "Woe is me for I am undone"; Job, the upright, said, "Behold I am vile"; and Paul, the chief of apostles, confessed, "I am the chief of sinners"; our blessed Lord stood at the grave of Lazarus, and said, "I am the Resurrection and the Life; he that believeth in Me, though he were dead, yet shall he live, and he that liveth and believeth in Me, shall never die."

These words of eternal life draw me to Him. They obliterate every other person from my soul's vision. They make hope gird on the pilgrim's attire. They bind us to His person. The dishonesty of infidels is the dishonesty of Pilate. The Roman governor repeatedly confessed, "I find no fault in Him," yet he scourged Him. He washed his hands, saying, "I am innocent of the blood of this just person, see ye to it," and yet he delivered Him to be crucified. Thus do unbelievers act still. They say the most flattering things of His words, and prophesy their continual triumph; and yet impeach Him in denying His Godhead, as one of the worst of men. Like the despisers of old, they wonder and perish. "Never man spake like this man," say they; but they spit in His face and nail Him to the cross. But Peters and Johns, Marthas and Marys, still sit at His feet, cherishing His words for His sake; and loving Him for His word's sake; confessing like the Bride, "His mouth is most sweet, yea, He is altogether lovely."

Though these gracious words of our Lord caused wonder and astonishment to His hearers in the synagogue at Nazareth, that wonder soon changed to indignation, as the grace of His words ran counter to their national prejudices. They were gracious words still, from His lips, when all those in the synagogue were filled with wrath. He had not changed to words of judgment. He was speaking gracious words still. The bringing up to their memories of the healing of the Gentile Naaman, and the blessing of the Gentile widow, in the days of Elijah, were intimations of the grace of God, bursting all barriers, and flowing out to lepers and widows everywhere. This grace was just as distasteful to the bigoted Israelites and the Pharisees, as were His words of denunciation and condemnation upon them for their hypocrisy and covetousness. The proud hearts of men have no appreciation for the gracious words of the Lord Jesus. But how those words have been treasured by the Naamans he has cleansed, and by the desolate ones to whom He has brought life and hope, as Elijah did to the Sidonian woman, who was gathering two sticks to make a little fire, and bake a little cake, before she and her son lay down to die.

The Gospels contain gracious words such as were never spoken by any other man; words that could not possibly come from any but God manifest in the flesh. What man could say, "Thy sins be forgiven thee," as Jesus did to the paralyzed man let down through the roof? (Lk. 5:20). Who but He could say, "Thy faith hath saved thee; go in peace," and "her sins which were many are forgiven," as He did to the notorious woman who kissed and anointed those blessed feet that followed until they found her? (Lk. 7:36-50). The Jews said, "Why doth this man thus speak blasphemies? Who can forgive sins but God only?" Those who were blessed by His words carried them in their hearts as their most treasured recollection, and would say with the officers, "Never man spake like this Man."

Blind Bartimeus; Zaccheus of the sycamore tree; Mary Magdalene, out of whom went seven demons; Peter, who said,

"Depart from me, for I am a sinful man, O Lord"; the woman of Samaria, whose life was laid bare at Sychar's well; and a host of others who heard and felt the humiliating, yet sanctifying and satisfying words of grace that came from His lips, knew beyond doubt that His words were the words of God. They felt like the friends of the bridegroom, when men had well drunk, looking at six water pots of the best wine—so much of the best, when they needed so little. They were like those among the five thousand who ate to satisfaction of the ever-increasing loaves and fishes till they were filled. So did sinners of every type drink the water of life, from His words; and felt there was wine and blessing from Him beyond their ability to appropriate. Enemies and friends alike knew Christ spoke gracious words. The rulers of the temple supposed His grace was in direct rebellion to the words of Moses, when they tested His orthodoxy in the temple, "Moses in the law commanded that such should be stoned but what sayest Thou?" They went out one by one, silent in their own guilt, but enemies to His grace still (Jn. 8:9).

It was when the Pharisees would advertise the attitude of the Lord to publicans and sinners, and place on His character the full vent of their displeasure: "This man receiveth sinners and eateth with them," that He spoke those gracious parabolic words of Luke 15; words that have cheered and charmed the people of God, and caused joy in heaven over sinners repenting, for almost nineteen centuries. As the sharp knife releases the myrrh from the tree of the wilderness, so did the contradiction of sinners continually press from our Lord the sweet savor of the grace and kindness of God.

To quote His gracious words would necessitate copying the whole of the gospel story. These gracious words are unlike what ever has, or ever could come, from the lips of a mere man. David showed grace to Mephibosheth, but it was the kindness of God. David could not say, "Come unto Me all ye that labor, and are heavy laden and *I* will give you rest"; or "He that drinketh of the water that *I* shall give him shall never thirst; for the water that I shall give him shall be in him a well of water springing up into everlasting life."

The unprejudiced heart of any honest man knows that the words of Christ were never imagined by any of the fallen sons of

Adam. They never could have been written but by inspiration of the Spirit of God; they never could have been spoken but by One who was God, as well as a man. Apart from all the difficulties that Christians and infidels have found, or invented, to confuse or deny inspiration of the Scriptures, the fact remains that we have in the Gospels the words of Christ; words that must have been spoken by Him.

Listen to His voice. Sit at the feet of the Lord like Mary and hear His words as He speaks to you. Like David, you will say, "His words are sweeter than honey and the honeycomb" (Ps. 19:10), or like the writer of Psalm 119, "The law of His mouth is better to me than thousands of gold and silver" (v. 72).

Men speak great swelling words of vanity, but pride and a haughty spirit ride only a few paces before a fall; then these loud utterances disappear like foam on the water. No other man has ever presumed to speak the language of Christ. His words are His glory. The wonderful words of Christ were easily understood. They were living, healthful words. Those who heard His words were either moved to wonder and worship or else to violent indignation and hate. His words breathed His deity. In the calmest and most peaceful spirit, He spoke the language of equality with God. With perfect freedom and unruffled self-possession, He poured out the truth of His exalted deity and of His gracious humanity. His words, like His person, united in one the glory of the Godhead and the gentleness of His unspotted humanity.

We add our simple testimony to the outspoken excuse of the Sanhedrin officers, "Never man spake like this Man."

CHAPTER FOUR

The Witness of His Works

"If I had not done among them the works which none other man did, they had not had sin: but now have they both seen and hated both Me and My Father" (Jn. 15:24).

"The works that I do in my Father's name, they bear witness of Me" (Jn. 10:25).

"The works which the Father hath given Me to finish, the same works that I do, bear witness of Me, that the Father hath sent Me" (Jn. 5:36).

What were these works of our Lord "which none other man did"? Moses healed a leprous woman (Num. 12:13); he did mighty signs in Egypt, even stretching his hand over the sea allowing the people of God through on dry ground (Ex. 14:21-22). Joshua led Israel on dry ground through the river Jordan (Josh. 3:9-17). Samuel called on the Lord and the Lord sent thunder and rain (1 Sam. 12:17-18). Elijah said to Ahab, "As the Lord God of Israel liveth, before whom I stand, there shall not be dew nor rain these years, but according to my word" (1 Ki. 17:1). Both Elijah and Elisha smote the waters of Jordan and parted them (2 Ki. 2:8-14). Elisha raised a dead child to life (2 Ki. 4:33-37). Elisha fed a hundred men with twenty loaves of bread (2 Ki. 4:42-44). A prophet healed Jeroboam's withered arm (1 Ki. 13:6).

What is the difference between these mighty works and the mighty works of the Lord Jesus? These Old Testament servants did their works to witness to another, to the Lord in fact. The mighty works that our Lord did were the works of God to give testimony to the Son. The works of Christ bore witness to Himself. Our Lord healed the impotent man at Bethesda by His word to show that He was the true "house of mercy," and that believing and hearing His word would bring life from the dead (see Jn. 5:24). Our Lord fed five thousand with five loaves and two little fishes to show that He was both "the Bread of God" and "the Bread of Life" (see Jn. 6:33, 48). He raised Lazarus to manifest that He was truly "the Resurrection and the Life" (Jn. 11:25); and that those who believed on Him, though they were dead, would yet live by His power.

The mighty works of our Lord bore witness of Him. They told what He was and what He was able to do for those who believed on His name. In this His works were different.

When He opened the eyes of one born blind, He said, "I am the light of the world" (Jn. 9:5). The stupendous work authenticated the stupendous claim. Christ the Lord forgave the sins of a paralyzed man, and then it is said, "But that ye may know that the Son of man hath power on earth to forgive sins, (He said unto the sick of the palsy) I say unto thee, Arise, and take up thy couch, and go into thine house" (Lk. 5:24).

Had our Lord not been what He was, He could not have done what He did. His works were unique; they were not only mighty works, they gave testimony to a Mighty Worker.

However, although our Lord did the works Himself, it is also true that the Father did them: "Believest thou not that I am in the Father, and the Father in Me? the words that I speak unto you I speak not of Myself: but the Father that dwelleth in Me, *He doeth the works*" (Jn. 14:10). Thus the works of our Lord revealed His oneness with the Father. In this way His works were the works "that none other man did."

Our Lord walked on the raging sea (Mt. 14:25-32). On another occasion He "rebuked the wind, and said unto the sea, Peace, be still. And the wind ceased and there was a great calm" (Mk. 4:39). In this way He showed that He was the One who "stilled the noise of the seas, the noise of their waves, and the tumult of the people" (Ps. 65:7).

He turned water into wine in Cana of Galilee, and "manifested forth *His glory*" (Jn. 2:11). Yet when Simon Magus would glorify himself, the offended Spirit of God condemned him to perdition immediately (see Acts 8:18-23). When Peter and John raised an impotent man, they said to the people, "Why look ye so earnestly on us, as though by our own power or holiness we had made this man to walk?" (Acts 3:12). When Paul and Barnabas were about to be worshiped because of the healing of the crippled man at Lystra (Acts 14:8-18), they ran among the people to restrain them from their purpose: "Sirs, why do ye these things? We also are men of like passions with you, and preach unto you that ye should turn from these vanities unto the living God, which made heaven, and earth, and the sea, and all things that are therein" (Acts 14:15).

Worship belonged only to the Creator. Paul and Barnabas would not allow this honor to be done to them. But the Lord Jesus accepted the worship of the blind man whose eyes He opened. "Jesus heard that they had cast him out; and when He had found him, He said unto him, Dost thou believe on the Son of God? He answered and said, Who is He, Lord, that I might believe on Him? And Jesus said unto him, Thou hast both seen Him, and it is He that talketh with thee. And he said, Lord I believe. And he worshiped Him" (Jn. 9:35-38). Our Lord accepted the worship of the Samaritan who was cleansed from his leprosy (see Lk. 17:15-17); also of a young ruler (see Mt. 9:18), and many others (see Mt. 2:11; 8:2; 14:33; 15:25; 28:9, 17, etc.).

It is important to note that His enemies acknowledged His works. When our Lord raised Lazarus to life at Bethany, the chief priests and Pharisees said, "What do we? For *this man doeth many miracles.* If we let Him thus alone, all men will believe on Him: and the Romans shall come and take away both our place and nation" (Jn. 11:47-48). The leaders of the nation acknowledged both the raising of Lazarus and all the other great miracles of the Lord. Incestuous Herod also acknowledged the mighty works of the Lord Jesus: "At that time Herod the tetrarch heard of the fame of Jesus, and said unto his servants, This is John the Baptist; he is risen from the dead; and therefore mighty works do show forth themselves in him" (Mt. 14:1-2). How few were honest and sincere as Nicodemus who came to Jesus by night and said, "Rabbi, we know that Thou art a teacher come from God; for no man can do these miracles that Thou doest except God be with him" (Jn. 3:2).

Some even doubted whether He did the miracles. Our Lord's brothers came to Him, and said, "Depart hence, and go into Judea, that Thy disciples also may see the works that Thou doest. For there is no man that doeth anything in secret, and he himself seeketh to be known openly. If Thou do these things, show Thyself to the world" (Jn. 7:3-4). The Spirit of God adds, "For neither did His brethren believe on Him."

There are then three great outstanding facts concerning the mighty works of the Lord Jesus:

1. They were revelations of His glory; they manifested the exalted nature of His person like the pure gold candlestick in the tabernacle, whose lamps were lit to "give light over against it" (Ex. 25:37, literally, over against the face of it). That precious and lovely vessel shed its light on the perfection of its own substance, and on the beautiful adorning of "almonds, buds and flowers." So Christ our Lord in His gracious works shed the light of revelation on Himself and His grace.

2. The mighty works of our Lord were the works of the Father who dwelt in Him. They told the secret that Christ and His Father were one (Jn. 10:30). They manifested that the Father was well pleased with all that the Son did. In this way our Lord stands supreme and alone of all the children of men, "A standard-bearer among ten thousand" (Song of Sol. 5:10). He is the One who is altogether lovely. Where men had grieved God in His heart (Gen. 6:6), the Lord Jesus caused the Father to say, "This is My beloved Son, in whom I am well pleased" (Mt. 3:17).

3. The mighty works of the Lord Jesus were done—and the record of them was written—for our blessing and salvation. "That ye might believe that Jesus is the Christ the Son of God: and that believing ye might have life through His name" (Jn. 20:31). This is the renown of His works; the glory that was revealed in them, the love of the Father for the Son that was manifested by them, and the grace and love toward you and me of which they are the imperishable evidence. Whether we think of His words or His works, He is "a plant of renown." He was raised up "for us" or He never would have been here in this cold, antagonistic world. Might the words of His lips and the works of His grace be our constant meditation.

CHAPTER FIVE

His Lowliness

"He humbled Himself...made Himself of no reputation" (Phil. 2:7-8).

"And he brought the ark into the tabernacle, and set up the veil of the covering, and covered the ark of the testimony; as the Lord commanded Moses" (Ex. 40:21).

"And thou shalt make curtains of goats' hair to be a covering upon the tabernacle...and thou shalt make a covering for the tent of rams' skins dyed red, and a covering above of badgers' skins" (Ex. 26:7, 14).

In the tabernacle, where "every whit" of it utters His glory (Ps. 29:9), the glory and the preciousness were completely covered. The veil had a definite reference to the shekinah glory that rested on the mercy seat of the ark of the covenant, for it was called "the veil of the covering."

The priest who daily ministered in the holy place could look up at the lovely curtains overhead and see cherubim of glory in the woven beauty of the blue and purple and scarlet. He could look forward to the veil and see the same cherubim of glory woven there; but the glory beyond the veil he could not see. The veil which represented the flesh of our Lord (Heb. 10:20) was a covering on the brightness of glory that resided in the innermost sanctuary. This all tells in a striking way the story of the hidden, and of the revealed glory of our Lord Jesus Christ.

It was impossible for the glory of Hebrews 1 to be seen by men in the person of Jesus of Nazareth. But it was there. "Who being the brightness of His glory, and the express image of His person, and upholding all things by the word of His power" (Heb. 1:3). This was the hidden glory of His person. The veil of His flesh covered this shekinah glory of Christ from men. His flesh was "the veil of the covering."

In the cherubim of glory were four distinct forms: (i) the face of a lion, (ii) the face of an ox, (iii) the face of a man, and (iv) the face of a flying eagle. These four were representations of the honors of Christ. He was the royal lion of Matthew's Gospel, the yoked servant from Mark's pen, the Son of Man in Luke's account, and the High and Lofty One in John's portrait. This is what the priest saw before and above him as he stood to worship or to minister in the holy place. In those curtains and in that veil the consecrated priest saw "His glory (full of grace and truth)." But the life that revealed His lovely glory covered, like the veil, the "glory" that was His "before the world was."

The whole story of Christ in the Gospels and in the Epistles of the New Testament is told in pictures in the books of Exodus and Leviticus in the Old Testament. No chapter is missing, no line is omitted; the whole story is told in the things Moses made as perfectly as in the things the apostles wrote. Moses, with Aholiab and Bezaleel, made with metals, with wood, and with embroidery, for the eye to see, the very same pattern of Christ and His work, as Matthew, with Paul, John and others, wrote for the heart to hear; so that those whose eyes are not blinded can clearly see that the one Spirit controlled both. The "salvation" of the New Testament in all its marvelous outworkings has its blueprints in the books Moses wrote in the wilderness. This is known best by those who with reverent minds have studied both the plans and the masterpiece. In the tabernacle not an item is superfluous and not a detail is omitted.

There was then a "veil of the covering" even for the privileged priest in the holy place. There was glory that was hidden even from him. He could see much, both before and above him, but beyond the veil was a glory he could not behold. The only one who beheld the inner glory was the High Priest once a year on the Day of Atonement; then the High Priest typified the Lord alone. So there was glory in Christ that only God could know. "No man knoweth the Son but the Father" (Mt. 11:27).

The veil of Christ's flesh was too substantial for the eyes of men to penetrate. They could see the glory in it but not the glory beyond it. We shall some day be in the presence of His glory, that glory which He had with the Father before the world was, but even then the glory we shall see will be the glory His Father has given to Him (Jn. 17:24).

The glory the disciples saw in His life was the moral glory of grace and truth. The glory that Peter, James, and John saw on the Mount of Transfiguration was the glory of His countenance and the glory of His garments (Lk. 9). We know there was a glory of His being, of the express image of God's person that was covered by the veil from the eyes of all men. That glory was too exalted for man to reach, too intense for us to look upon.

The glories that priests could see were covered from the outside. Above the beautiful curtains called the tabernacle was a covering of curtains of goats' hair. It was a scape-goat that carried away the sins of the people on the Day of Atonement; there was also a goat that died on that day (Lev. 16:15).

Above the covering of the tent of goat's hair was a covering of rams' skins dyed red. This ram was the "ram of consecration" (Lev. 8:22). These skins would never have been red had they not been dyed. The red of blood shedding was on the skins that covered the tent of the tabernacle. Above the covering of rams' skins dyed red was a covering of badgers' skins.

Thus the glory was covered, covered, covered, till from the outside it was without form or comeliness. The outside covering is called badgers' skins, but no one today knows for certainty what kind of common covering that outside one of the tabernacle was. There are as many opinions as there were concerning Christ in the days of His flesh, or as there are of Christ among men today. Those outside skins were the final covering of His glory under the form of a servant as He appeared in the likeness of men. This then is the true picture of what God delights in— covered glory. It is glory that can only be found by finding God. It is glory that can only be seen by coming as a sinner to the altar and to the laver through the door.

In Christ on earth there was covered glory. He could no more lay aside His glory than I could lay aside my heart or my personality. He covered His glory. For thirty years in Nazareth there lived in a Man perfect obedience and perfect submission to God. That Man was Jehovah's fellow. That lowly, laboring One was the Creator of all, God's only Son. He was without honor among men. Not a shred of blue, purple, or scarlet was seen, nothing but badgers' skins. Even Mary and Joseph had looked so long on the humble exterior that they seemed to have forgotten what the angels of heaven had gloriously announced at His birth. His brethren could not understand why nothing should be said or done till He was thirty years of age. He never once declared His pre-incarnate glory to them. So there was not a single revelation of the glory of the tabernacle; the badgers' skins covered all.

This was what pleased God. When He who was higher than the angels was made in the likeness of men, He acted so differently from all others. When men coveted glory that they could not attain, and tried to parade glory they did not possess, the Lord Jesus completely covered all the glory that was His to be unnoticed in the world. This is how He humbled Himself. This is why God has highly exalted Him.

There is too much paraded glory today. Too many men and women want to show themselves to the world. For men to display their own glory is not glory. Lovely grace hides its beauty that it may only be betrayed by its fragrance. Our Lord never sought a crowd. Like charity, He vaunted not Himself. Christ had no one campaign for Him. There was no stage and no glamor. Herod might have wondered if he had seen a miracle performed by Him. But the way of God is not the way of man. When God gave a manifestation of that which delighted His heart, it is pictured in the Tabernacle and seen in the life and death of our Lord Jesus Christ.

The One who was crucified in *weakness*; the One who for us became *poor*; the One who never paraded His wisdom; the One who was forsaken; the One who bore the deepest shame and curse; the One who was hated without a cause, is the One who alone is worthy to receive "power and riches and wisdom and strength and honor and glory and blessing." The world showed its utter estrangement from God in that it never attributed any of these honors to Him. The world today shows its besotted ignorance in that this covered glory of heaven's lovely Man is still detested and unknown.

CHAPTER SIX

The Renown of His Ways

"I have raised him up in righteousness, and I will direct all his ways: he shall build my city, and he shall let go my captives, not for price nor reward, saith the Lord of hosts" (Isa. 45:13).

Our Lord was like wisdom. His ways were ways of pleasantness, and all His paths were peace (Prov. 3:17). The world He had made, and the world in which He was, knew Him not; but He was the delight of the heart of God. God said from heaven, "This is My beloved Son, in whom I am well pleased." Not only when He went down into the waters of baptism, but also when He was on the Mount of Transfiguration with Moses and Elijah, or surrounded by publicans and sinners, was He God's delight.

The meal offering of Leviticus 2 suggests the lovely perfections of the ways of our Lord. That offering was composed of fine flour mingled and anointed with oil, with frankincense upon it. The flour was the best—all good for food; the oil was the best of the olives that made man's face to shine; the pure frankincense was the most fragrant possible. This was God's own picture of the delightful moral perfections of Christ. The meal offering was food of God and of the priests. Part was burned on the altar and part was the portion of Aaron and his sons.

No tongue could possibly describe the delight of the heart of God in that lowly life lived in the seclusion of Nazareth. God, who alone knew the glory which that humble form covered, alone could appreciate the path of lowly obedience He took.

Little is said in the Gospel records of those thirty quiet years. The little things that are said are windows opened for a moment to reveal the light and loveliness that most of the time was hidden under that form of a servant.

The prophet Isaiah gives us one brief look at Him in 53:2, "He shall grow up before Him as a tender plant." That plant was not tender in that it was likely to perish in the cold of this foreign world, but tender like an exotic that feels the change of the climate from which it came.

This is how He grew up before the Lord. Not a day, not a moment in Nazareth that God did not look down from heaven with delight upon Him. No husbandman ever watched a rare and lovely plant as God did His delightful Son. There was death and corruption all around; but there was life and holiness in Him. The world was full of striving, lusting men and women, crushing and climbing to excel; here was One who took the lowest place and grew unknown but to God alone.

That Babe in the manger was God manifest in the flesh. The One His virgin mother held at her breast was the Mighty One who upholds all things. The shining glory was hidden, but the glory of grace and truth was beautifully revealed.

How wonderful that a lad in a peasant home in Nazareth, eating common food, sleeping on a hard bed, working with His hands as soon as He was able, that that One should be the very Son of God! "The only begotten of the Father, full of grace and truth." This was the way of God. These were the ways of Christ. Pure and fragrant like a lily among the thorns; rare beauty for only God to appreciate; growing up before the Lord as a tender plant. To Israel He was a root out of a dry ground. He had no form nor comeliness to them.

In Luke 2:52, there is another touching and exquisite reference to the youth of Christ: "And Jesus increased in wisdom and stature, and in favor with God and man." He did not seem to be a prodigy. The lovely ways of a perfect child characterized His childhood years. The wisdom of His words increased according to His stature. As a youth He did not speak as a patriarch. His life was unblemished and altogether lovely, but it was consistent with His years and humble circumstances.

The very covering with silence of those years at Nazareth is the perfect way of the Spirit of God. This was His way. There was no outshining of His glory. There was no demonstration of His miraculous greatness. The home was humble; its furnishings almost nil, no doubt; the table was not the table of a king; but there the loveliest flower that ever graced this earth grew unnoticed by all but God.

Luke reminds us He "was subject unto [Mary and Joseph]" (Lk. 2:51). This was another way of loveliness in Him as a child of twelve years. After the episode in the temple, and His gentle reproof, "Know ye not that I must be about My Father's business?" it is recorded that He went down with Joseph and Mary, "and came to Nazareth, and was subject unto them." He declared that God was His Father, and that His business was all-important to Him, but nevertheless recognized His earthly relationship and was subject to Joseph and Mary. That subjection of His own voluntary will was lovely in Him. Joseph and Mary had the manifest token that He fully comprehended His Sonship of God and His exalted mission, but that did not change His moral perfection as subject to those to whose care God had entrusted Him. This one incident when He was twelve years of age is on record to reveal the consistent moral perfection of our Lord as He grew up in the family of Joseph the carpenter.

When our Lord was "sitting in the midst of the doctors" (Lk. 2:46) in the temple, He, again like charity, did not behave Himself unseemly (1 Cor. 13:5). He was "hearing them, and asking them questions." It does not say, He was teaching them or answering their questions. He did not pose as a teacher, though there dwelt in Him "all the treasures of wisdom and knowledge" (Col. 2:3). "All that heard Him were astonished at His understanding and answers." He was the true speaker of Psalm 119:99, "I have more understanding than all my teachers: for Thy testimonies are my meditation." All His life, Isaiah 50:4 was true of Him: "He wakeneth morning by morning, He wakeneth mine ear to hear as the learned." Thus, His childhood and youth were passed in quiet, loving fellowship with God; hearing His voice and responding to His love.

"Be pitiful, be courteous" (1 Pet. 3:8), enjoins the apostle who seemingly had to learn it the hard way. Our Lord was very pitiful, and always courteous. There is the thought of offense latent in each of these words; "pitiful," "courteous." Pitiful is that condition of soul that considers the weakness, the infirmity, or ignorance of the offender, and thus does not take offense. This was always true of our Lord. There was compassion and mercy always in His heart. He considered the burden of others.

The story is told of Napoleon walking with a lady along a path that became so narrow that the lady had to walk ahead with the Emperor behind. Approaching them was a workman with a heavy load on his back. The lady kept to the path so the burdened workman would have to step aside. Napoleon gently took the lady by the shoulders and caused her to leave the path so the man with the load could continue on the walk. Speaking to the lady, Napoleon said, "Madame, consider the burden."

This our Lord always did. The disciples rudely awakened Him from His sleep when He was weary in the boat on stormy Galilee: "Master, carest Thou not that we perish?" What unbelieving folly (except that we are guilty of the same!) to suppose that the boat would sink with Christ in it. But He considered their panic and fear, and rebuked the wind and the sea with, "Peace, be still." He could have rebuked them and let the storm rage on. But He was pitiful.

When He, their Lord, was praying more earnestly in Gethsemane because of the coming cross with all its terror, He said, "My soul is exceeding sorrowful unto death: tarry ye here, and watch" (Mk. 14:34). If ever He desired the sympathy of loving human hearts, it was then. His sweat was, as it were, great drops of blood falling down to the ground. But when He came from prayer, the three favored disciples were asleep. "What, could ye not watch with Me one hour? Watch and pray, that ye enter not into temptation," He warned them. He went away and prayed again. When He returned to them, they were asleep again. Then He said, "The spirit indeed is willing, but the flesh is weak." How pitiful that was! He seemed to say, "They were willing to watch with Me but they were not able." How gracious of Him to remember the weakness of the flesh!

At Calvary, when our Lord suffered the repeated abuse and mortification of the shame men heaped on Him, He said, "Father, forgive them; for they know not what they do" (Lk. 23:34). Rotherham's translation says, "He kept saying, Father,

forgive them, for they know not what they do." He was suffering the cruel, heartless infliction of crucifixion; yet He could
remember their ignorance and plead it to His Father for their
forgiveness. No doubt many of the perpetrators of Calvary will
be in heaven in answer to that prayer.

He was that charity which "suffers long, and is kind" (1 Cor.
13:4). How wonderful that His spirit never soured. How perfectly lovely of Him to "endure all things" without for one moment
either doubting God's love, or threatening His persecutors! The
fountain of His heart's love could not be stopped. He not only
suffered long, but even in extremity He was still kind.

He was always courteous. Behind this word "courteous" is
the thought of not giving offense. Our Lord was so thoughtful
and so careful to give no offense. In the house of Simon the
Pharisee, when our Lord was so discourteously received by His
host, He was most courteous. Simon had nothing for Christ; no
kiss; no water for His feet; no oil for His head; nothing to give
Him, because nothing had been received from Him. There was
no love at all, because there had been no forgiveness.

The woman was such a contrast. She loved much and she
showed it. She washed His feet with her tears. She kissed His
feet, and anointed them with ointment. Simon looked sullenly
on: "A woman like that I would not allow to touch me! He surely does not know her character. If He were a prophet He would
know." So Simon mused.

"Simon, I have somewhat to say unto thee." Then Simon
found that He read his heart as well as He knew the character of
the woman! But see the courtesy of the parable of the two
debtors, the one who owed fifty pence, and the other five hundred; the one who loved little, and the other loved much. Was
this Simon and the woman? It was the woman, all right. She
loved much. She was forgiven much. But it was not Simon. He
had no love. He had been forgiven nothing. What a courteous
way to omit mention of the one who had been forgiven nothing
and so had no love! Simon could read himself into the picture.
Then, "Thou gavest Me no kiss: thou gavest Me no water for My
feet: My head with oil thou didst not anoint." The woman gave
Christ everything, but Simon gave Him nothing. Still our Lord
was courteous even with His most discourteous of His enemies.

"Go and sit down in the lowest room" (Lk. 14:10). Where was our Lord sitting when He gave these instructions to His disciples? Although higher than the highest, our Lord sat in the lowest rooms. No one estimated His worth accurately. The ruler did not say to Him, "Friend, go up higher." God surely did, and will, but man did not. They just let Him sit in the lowest room. What courtesy on His part! Courtesy that could not possibly offend any. No one could envy Him. He was that charity that "envieth not" and that "vaunteth not itself, is not puffed up."

This was His perfect way to "make Himself of no reputation" and take the lowest place of all. Being in the lowest room, our Lord was near the man who needed Him; the man who had the dropsy or edema (Lk. 14:2-4). Sitting in the lowest room, our Lord dispensed the greatest blessing!

In the home of His special friends at Bethany, how courteously He behaved. Remember the occasion when Martha was cumbered about much serving. She looked with impatient eye on Mary "sitting at Jesus feet": "Lord, dost Thou not care that my sister hath left me to serve alone? Bid her therefore that she help me." But that would have been out of place for Him as a guest to take the place of master in the house of His friends. Martha wanted Him to assume the role of head of that house, but He was too courteous to leave the character of guest.

He was charity that did not "behave itself unseemly." Although Lord of all, He respected the honor of His friends ruling in their own house. But He did give Martha needed instruction as to what delighted Him most. He did not desire to sit alone while both the sisters busied themselves preparing Him many dishes. The Word of God was more to Him than His necessary food. When the care of "many things" took the place of hearing His Word, it is the "many things" that must go. So our Lord, when a guest, maintained the character of a guest, and did it in a lovely way. He was the courteous Gentleman in the home.

There are three classes of outcasts appearing again and again on the pages of the Gospel story. They are: Samaritans—hated because of their history and competitive religion; publicans—hated by the Jews for their practices of farming the taxes and exploiting the people; and sinners—despised because of the self-righteousness of the Pharisees. Our Lord's way with these brought Him opprobrium and shame from the bigoted leaders of the nation. Yet His ways were ways of grace.

It was a Samaritan woman who said, "The Jews have no dealings with the Samaritans" (Jn. 4:9). This was the reason she wondered why this Jewish Stranger should ask a drink of her at Sychar's well. Even the disciples felt this was exceeding what was right and proper, to talk to a woman of Samaria. They "marveled that He talked with the woman: yet no man said, What seekest thou? or Why talkest thou with her?" (Jn. 4:27). Evidently they wanted to ask Him those very questions but were reluctant to do it. Thus it was that the great subject of worship in spirit and truth was revealed at Sychar to the woman of Samaria. Grace in Him knew no restrictions and looked not for worthy objects on which to bestow its richest gifts.

The Lord did not act on the prejudices of the Samaritans, for when He was going to Jerusalem He sent His disciples to prepare Him a place in a village of Samaria (Lk. 9:51-52). The violation of the Jewish procedure caused Him to be slandered as a Samaritan. "Thou art a Samaritan and hast a devil" (Jn. 8:48). His violation of the Samaritan prejudice in going to Jerusalem to the feast and passing through their country caused them to refuse to receive Him (Lk. 9:53). The Jewish reproach He accepted, for in a parable He called Himself "a certain Samaritan" (Lk. 10:33). The Samaritans' rejection because of their prejudice did not dry up His springs of grace, for immediately on leaving Samaria He healed a Samaritan leper (Lk. 17:16). It was the same journey mentioned in the 9th and 17th chapters of Luke.

In the life of our Lord He ran counter to every prejudice in Judea, Samaria, and Galilee. There was religious pride in each place. The humbling of this pride caused bitterness in the hearts of those whose bigotry was opposed. That bitterness and opposition never lessened the grace in the heart of Him who went about doing good.

Reading Luke 9 after John 4 reveals that, although grace may make many converts in a place ("many believed on Him"), deep rooted religious tradition will likely remain. Many Samaritans believed on Christ as the Messiah, but Samaritans would not tolerate a setting of Jerusalem feasts above their worship. They would even refuse Christ when His face was as though He were going to Jerusalem. I suppose the very early honoring of the mountain of Samaria would be ample justification for Samaritans looking on this as the right place. Many a book could be written (and probably was) about the comparative claims of Jerusalem and Gerizim as the place where men ought to worship. The place was all important in their eyes. Instead of a place, worship now is in spirit and in truth. What is important today is not the place but the way. "After the way which they call heresy, so worship I the God of my fathers" (Acts 24:14). The Acts of the Apostles never honors "the place," but "the way." The place usually refers to the temple. The word "way" is used for Christianity and the truth of God.

When because of His grace to the Samaritans the Jews said, "Thou art a Samaritan, and hast a devil" (Jn. 8:48), our Lord answered, "I have not a devil; but I honor My Father, and ye do dishonor Me." He would not say, "I am not a Samaritan," for such a statement might have offended the Samaritans. He was too courteous to give offense. Grace continually flowed from His lips in spite of the reproach it often brought to Him.

One of our Lord's chief disciples was a publican—"Matthew the publican." I have often wondered if Matthew were that publican who went behind the Pharisee to the temple to pray (Lk. 18:10-14): who smote upon his breast saying, "God, be merciful to me a sinner." Had this taken place in the life of Matthew before the Lord called him, it is no wonder he was singled out with the words, "Follow Me" (Mt. 9:9). The fact that a publican was chosen to write the Gospel of Christ the King, is surely the way of grace that completely ignored the reproach of men.

When publicans sat down to eat with the Lord, the scribes and Pharisees found fault: "Why do ye eat and drink with publicans and sinners?" The Lord justified Himself as the physician seeking the sick rather than those who thought they needed Him not (Lk. 5:27-32). The "gospel" according to the Pharisees— "This man receiveth sinners and eateth with them"—was spoken when "publicans and sinners drew near to hear Him" (Lk. 15:1-2). Then our Lord spoke those inimitable parables of the lost things and their finding. The ways of the Lord were always ways of grace and truth. He never sought the approbation of men. In a proud world among a proud people, the Son of God walked a path of unprecedented lowliness and grace.

When the impotent man was healed at the pool of Bethesda (Jn. 5), the Jews interrogated the happy, healed man carrying his bed home on his back, "What man is that which said unto thee, Take up thy bed, and walk?" The man did not even know His name! It says, "Jesus had conveyed Himself away, a multitude being in that place" (Jn. 5:13). How unlike the ways of men who crave all the publicity which exploits will bring to them.

God had said of old, "My ways are not your ways" (Isa. 55:8). It was true of the Lord Jesus; the ways of men were not His ways. Men thought little of God in heaven or of what would be pleasing to Him. This was everything to Christ our Lord. He did everything that pleased the Father. The Father's Name, the Father's kingdom, and the Father's will were the great dominating motives of the life of our Lord. He cared for nothing else.

CHAPTER SEVEN

Unique in His Death

Other men die because they have to die. Our Lord laid down His life of His own voluntary will. "I am the good shepherd: the good shepherd *giveth His life* for the sheep" (Jn. 10:11). "As the Father knoweth Me, even so know I the Father: and I *lay down My life* for the sheep" (Jn. 10:15). "Therefore doth My Father love Me, because I *lay down My life* that I might take it again. No man taketh it from Me, but I *lay it down of Myself.* I have power to lay it down, and I have power to take it again. This commandment have I received of My Father" (Jn. 10:17-18).

The very first prophecy of Christ suggested His death. God said to Satan in Eden when announcing the coming of the Conquering Seed, "It shall bruise thy head, and thou shalt bruise His heel" (Gen. 3:15).

The words of this promise probably seemed obscure to Adam and to his wife; but the subsequent unfoldings of Scripture show plainly that this first prophecy of Christ foretold His death.

Our Lord also "accomplished" His death. When Peter, James, and John were with the Lord in "the holy mount," Luke records: "Behold there talked with Him two men, which were Moses and Elias; who appeared in glory, and spoke of His decease which He should *accomplish* at Jerusalem" (Lk. 9:30-31).

Moses had a remarkable death; God was his undertaker. Yet Moses did not "accomplish" his decease. The word "accomplish" does not fit any other death but the death of Christ. Death is the invasion of the territory of a man by an enemy. The best of men, when they died, were said to give up the ghost, and to be gathered to their fathers; when they could live no longer, they succumbed to death. The death of the Lord Jesus was altogether different; it was perhaps the greatest of all His works.

The Greek word translated "accomplish" has a great latitude of meaning. Dr. James Strong in his concordance defines the word "accomplish" in this way. *Pleroo* —"to make replete, i.e. (lit.) to cram (a net), level up (a hollow), or (fig.) to furnish (or imbue, diffuse, influence), satisfy, execute (an office), finish (a period or task), verify (or coincide with a prediction), etc." All these defining words are full of meaning when applied to the death of the Lord Jesus. He cried, "It is finished" when He bowed His head in death. His death made all His work replete. A net crammed with fishes is the perfect satisfaction of the fisherman, the fullness of the expectation of his toil; so was the death of our Lord.

The death of Christ leveled up the hollows, when every valley was exalted, and a highway prepared for God and for His people. His death provided the only title and fitness for sinners to come to God. The blood of Christ is a perfect satisfaction for any sinner who will only trust it for cleansing and salvation. The death of Christ was the fulfillment of His office of Redeemer; it finished that period of "looking for redemption in Jerusalem"; it was the grand finishing of the work the Father gave Him to do; and that work alone verified the Old Testament prophecies by coinciding so perfectly with all that was written in the law and in the prophets and in the psalms concerning Him.

No other word could have been found to so strikingly present our Lord's work in His death as this word "accomplish."

Nothing could afford such a subject for conversation between Him and those heavenly visitors for that brief moment of His glory on the mount, but the subject of "His decease which He should accomplish at Jerusalem." What a thrilling subject it must have been! Usually the death of a man is his greatest defeat; the death of our Saviour was His greatest victory.

God commanded Abraham to offer his son Isaac on the altar as a test of Abraham's love and obedience; but the Father commanded His beloved Son to die the death of the cross. What glorious obedience was this that He "became obedient unto death, even the death of the cross" (Phil. 2:8). Such a commandment

76

could never have been given to a creature. The commandment to die for the sheep was given by the Father to the Son. "I lay down My life for the sheep…This commandment have I received of My Father" (Jn. 10:15, 18). When the Lord Jesus entered the world, He said, "Lo, I come to do Thy will, O God" (Heb. 10:9). When our Lord came to Gethsemane, the words of Isaiah the prophet were fulfilled, "The Lord God hath opened Mine ear, and I was not rebellious, neither turned away back. I gave My back to the smiters, and My cheeks to them that plucked off the hair: I hid not My face from shame and spitting" (Isa. 50:5-6). What confidence the Father must have had in the Son's love and faithfulness to give Him such a commandment as this! What love the Son must have had for the Father, to bear at His commandment the curse and death of the cross!

On the cross our Lord sustained God's wrath against sin; on the tree, He "was made a curse for us" (Gal. 3:13); in those hours of Calvary's darkness, the Christ of God was forsaken (Mt. 27:46). Hear the words of Scripture: *"Thy wrath* lieth hard upon Me, and Thou hast afflicted Me with all Thy waves" (Ps. 88:7). *"Thy fierce wrath* goeth over Me; Thy terrors have cut Me off" (Ps. 88:16). "Is it nothing to you, all ye that pass by? Behold and see if there be any sorrow like unto My sorrow, which is done unto Me, wherewith *the Lord hath afflicted Me* in the day of His fierce anger. *From above hath He sent fire into My bones* and it prevaileth against them" (Lam. 1:12-13).

This is what death meant to the Lord Jesus Christ: made a curse; visited with the wrath of God against sin; in darkness, forsaken, and alone, He died for us. As another has said, "Utterly solitary He died that none of us might have to face death alone." Or as we often sing,

> "Crowned with thorns upon the tree;
> Silent in Thine agony;
> Dying crushed beneath the load,
> Of the wrath and curse of God."

This was the heart-breaking anguish of His death. God left Him alone in the hour of His deepest suffering. Never in his day had David seen the righteous forsaken. The sorrowing One of Psalm 22 pleaded, "Our fathers trusted in Thee: they trusted and

Thou didst deliver them. They cried unto Thee and were delivered: they trusted in Thee and were not confounded. But I am a worm and no man; a reproach of men and despised of the people" (Ps. 22:4-6). The One who was the most faithful and the most beloved was the first to know the bitter sorrow of being left alone by God in the hour of His deep distress.

The honor of Christ's Person gave infinite value to His sufferings. The pain of His obedience made the preciousness of that loving surrender to the will of God of supremely greater worth and richer fragrance. When He who became a servant, of His own unfettered will showed His love and submission to God's word and at such tremendous cost to Himself as He did at Calvary, how gloriously precious it was! The death of God's saints had always been precious in His sight (Ps. 116:15), but never had there been a death that so filled the heart of God with unspeakable satisfaction as the death of Him who hung in blood and shame on the cross at Golgotha.

What a combining of defeat and victory, of disappointment and glory, that death was! The first verses of Isaiah 49 speak plainly of the life and death of Christ. Those verses clearly reveal the disappointment of our Lord over Israel not being gathered. Not discouragement, but disappointment. Hear our Lord say in prophecy in verse 4, "Then I said, I have labored in vain, I have spent My strength for nought and in vain: yet surely My judgment is with the Lord, and My work with My God." Then notice the answer of the Father to Him in the verse that follows: "And now, saith the Lord that formed Me from the womb to be His servant, to bring Jacob again to Him, Though Israel be not gathered, yet shall I be glorious in the eyes of the Lord, and My God shall be My strength." Read also verses 6 and 7. All the rest of that chapter is taken up with a detailed prophecy of all the blessed results of the cross and death of Christ that seemed so disappointing.

Yes, He who died at Calvary was "glorious in the eyes of the Lord," and He is God's "salvation unto the ends of the earth" (vv. 5-6).

This is another peculiar glory of the death of Christ. He died as a sacrifice for the sins of His people! "He was wounded for our transgressions, He was bruised for our iniquities: the chastisement of our peace was upon Him; and with His stripes we are healed" (Isa. 53:5). "All we like sheep have gone astray; we have turned every one to his own way; and the Lord hath laid on Him the iniquity of us all" (Isa. 53:6). "When He had by Himself purged our sins, [He] sat down on the right hand of the Majesty on high" (Heb. 1:3). "Who His own self bare our sins in His own body on the tree" (1 Pet. 2:24). "Christ died for our sins according to the Scriptures; and...He was buried, and...He rose again the third day according to the Scriptures" (1 Cor. 15:3-4).

Zelophehad, and every other son of Adam "died in his own sin" (Num. 27:3); but our Lord "did no sin" (1 Pet. 2:22), and "knew no sin" (2 Cor. 5:21), but was "holy, harmless, undefiled, separate from sinners, and made higher than the heavens" (Heb. 7:26). He never earned death, the wages of sin (Rom. 6:23). When He died, He gave Himself "for our sins" (Gal. 1:4), and "redeemed us from the curse of the law, being made a curse for us" (Gal. 3:13).

The guilt of the death of Christ lies heavily on Israel but responsibility is shared by the whole world of rebel sinners. When sentence was pronounced on Christ, Pilate the judge first proclaimed the innocence of the accused and then condemned Him to the most horrible and most shameful death that diabolical wickedness ever invented. What a travesty of justice this was! Did any court of any land ever treat an accused person so unjustly?

Our Lord thought of others with compassion when crushed, cursed, and dying. In prophecy it was written of Him, "Let not them that wait on Thee, O Lord God of hosts, be ashamed for my sake: let not those that seek Thee be confounded for my sake, O God of Israel. Because for Thy sake I have borne reproach; shame hath covered my face" (Ps. 69:6-7).

How gracious of that holy Sufferer to have such a concern as this for His disciples in the hours of His deepest agony and reproach! See the tender regard of His heart for His mother and for the women with her: "Now there stood by the cross of Jesus His mother, and His mother's sister, Mary the wife of Cleophas, and Mary Magdalene" (Jn. 19:25). How His tender feelings of love and sympathy went out for His mother! He understood the "sword" that was "piercing her own soul also," and showed His deep concern for her. "When Jesus therefore saw His mother, and the disciple standing by, whom He loved, He saith unto His mother, Woman, behold thy Son! Then saith He to the disciple, Behold thy mother! And from that hour that disciple took her unto his own home" (Jn. 19:26-27).

Mary did not linger to see the death of Him who had brought such joy to her heart. At the Lord's bidding, John took her away before He bowed His head upon the tree. Not only did our Lord think of His disciples and His mother, He even thought mercifully of His bitter enemies. Immediately following the account of the worst that His enemies did to Him in Luke's Gospel, you have the words of the intercession of our Lord for them. "And when they came to the place, which is called Calvary, there they crucified Him, and the malefactors, one on the right hand, and the other on the left. Then said Jesus, Father, forgive them; for they know not what they do" (Lk. 23:33-34).

Those who sat around the cross to watch the Saviour die thought that His death was His utter and irretrievable defeat. Our Lord had said, "Verily, verily, I say unto you, That ye shall weep and lament, but the world shall rejoice: and ye shall be sorrowful, but your sorrow shall be turned into joy" (Jn. 16:20).

The cross for the time blasted all the hopes of the chosen disciples; they forsook Him and fled. They mourned and wept, hiding away for fear of the Jews. Some were so filled with black despair that even the report of His resurrection did not sufficiently interest them to take them to the grave to see for themselves. They turned their backs sadly on Jerusalem and went home to Emmaus. The companionable Stranger who walked with them made their heart burn within them as He opened to them the Scriptures. Complete despair so filled their spirits that they even told this Stranger of the witness of the angels to the women at the grave, and ended with the hopeless words, "but Him they saw not."

Calculating Thomas, guileless Nathaniel, outspoken Peter, devoted John, and all the others of the twelve with the women of His acquaintance looked on the cross, where Christ was so shamefully crucified, as His collapse and defeat. They could not see His death in any other light. It was an immeasurable sorrow to them. It blasted hope and joy from every heart.

The taunts and jeers of our Lord's enemies while He hung forsaken on that middle cross, showed that they were completely satisfied that this was to Him the end of His words and His works. More absolute helplessness they could not conceive. Without a friend to espouse His cause; without a follower bold enough to fight for Him; and without an acquaintance loyal enough to acknowledge His name in the hour of His rejection—it looked like the most heart-rending defeat any leader could possibly suffer.

But instead of defeat, the death of Christ was the grandest and most complete victory ever won. Evidences of that triumph began to follow each other in rapid succession. Even before He died, supernatural darkness spread over the land. Then when the Saviour cried aloud, "It is finished," the earth quaked and the rocks rent like an old garment when it is torn by a mighty hand.

Then Joseph and Nicodemus came and gave Him the burial of a king. With all their hate and exasperation, the priests and elders of the Jews were not able to hinder the loving service to Him of these two Sanhedrin counselors. The consternation of the Jewish leaders must have resembled that of Haman of old when he had to walk the streets of Shushan with Mordecai, the man he hated, riding on the king's mule, while he cried, "Thus shall it be done to the man whom the king delighteth to honor." In the end, Haman died on the very gallows he built for the man he despised and hated.

It was exactly so in this case. Both the devil and the servants he employed to hasten the Christ of God to a malefactor's cross shall find in that cross their eternal undoing and destruction. It is written in the Scriptures of the victory of Calvary: "Forasmuch as the children are partakers of flesh and blood, He also Himself likewise took part of the same; that through death He might destroy him that had the power of death, that is the devil; and deliver them who through fear of death were all their lifetime subject to bondage" (Heb. 2:14-15).

Before the resurrection of Christ, death seems to have been like a walled city with inpenetrable gates, and with the devil holding the keys of that city. No one had been able to break that stronghold. "The power of death" was in the hand of our enemy.

Our Lord was "crucified through weakness" (2 Cor. 13:4); it was the love and obedience of the Lord Jesus that held Him a dying Saviour to the cross. In those dread hours men and the devil did their worst to Him. There was no restraint on the hatred and cruelties of wicked men. God in heaven left Christ alone to die. He did not come down from the cross, though priests and malefactors challenged Him to do so. They all concluded He was not the Son of God, and that He could not come down. The devil knew well who He was, but in his consummate pride, he imagined that he had the Prince of Life entirely in his power. Satan felt like the Philistine Gazites when Samson, the mighty man of Israel, was in their walled city with its gates and bars (Jud. 16:2-3). They said, "In the morning when it is day, we shall kill him" (Jud. 16:2). The Philistines never dreamed there was the possibility of their prisoner escaping in the night time. The mighty Samson lifted gates, bars, posts and all on his powerful shoulders and carried them to the top of a hill that "is before Hebron." Hebron was the place where Caleb dispossessed the Anakims, and where later David was crowned king.

Our Lord entered the devil's stronghold when He entered death. Satan discovered that He who seemed so helpless on the cross was the "Lord strong and mighty" when He passed into the nether regions. "Through death He destroyed him that had the power of death." The devil was spoiled of all his weapons and armor. When, in resurrection, our Lord came out of the city of death, He carried gates, bars, posts and all to the top of a hill. All the powers of darkness will never be able to carry them back again. Like Gaza, after Samson's humbling of her pride, death after the victory of our Redeemer was left without its gates of brass and without its bars of iron. The keys of hell and of death were in the hands of the Lord Jesus when He spoke to John in resurrection: "I am He that liveth, and was dead; and behold, I am alive for evermore, Amen; and have the keys of hell and of death" (Rev. 1:18).

The death of the Lord Jesus was a glorious victory. He "spoiled principalities and powers, He made a show of them openly, triumphing over them in it" (Col. 2:15). When prophets or kings died, their work was done, but the evidences of the invincible might of our Lord were never manifest till then in all their conquering and delivering power. It was noticed by the rabbis long ago, and it baffled their understanding, that most of the glorious deeds of Messiah recorded in Isaiah 53 come after the mentioning of His death in verse 10. How could He "see His seed?" How could He "prolong His days?" How could "the pleasure of the Lord prosper in His hand" after His death? How could He "see of the travail of His soul and be satisfied?" How could He "divide the spoil with the strong," after He had died? It was a problem without a solution to those who rejected the death and resurrection of Messiah.

Again, that chapter in Isaiah's prophecy (ch. 49) that contains the account of Messiah's disappointment over Israel not being gathered (v. 5), contains this question also, "Shall the prey be taken from the mighty, or the lawful captive delivered?" (v. 24). The answer is given immediately, "But thus saith the Lord, Even the captives of the mighty shall be taken away, and the prey of the terrible shall be delivered" (v. 25). Thus even in the Old Testament Scriptures the victory of the death of our Lord Jesus Christ is found.

The blessed application of the death and resurrection of Christ to the nation of Israel in the day of its restoration is expressed by the prophet in these words, "He will swallow up death in victory" (Isa. 25:8). This again is enlarged in Hosea 13:14, "I will ransom them from the power of the grave. I will redeem them from death: O death, I will be thy plagues; O grave, I will be thy destruction."

Before Israel knows the redemption of Messiah's victory as foretold in these thrilling words, we who are of the Church of Christ shall first enter the glory of it as is declared in 1 Corinthians 15:51-57. Then our happy hearts will shout for joy: "O death, where is thy sting? O grave, where is thy victory? The sting of death is sin; and the strength of sin is the law. But thanks be to God, who giveth us the victory through our Lord Jesus Christ." This jubilant and triumphant song of praise belongs to that blissful moment for which the church of Christ is waiting, even the moment of the redemption of our bodies at His coming.

The resurrection of God's saints at the coming of the Lord to the air (1 Thess. 4:17), and the gathering and restoration of Israel

at His appearing, will be most blessed and glorious manifesta-
tions of the victory of Immanuel at Jerusalem, in His death and
resurrection. It was then He gained the victory. It was He alone
who there and then fought that battle that will never have to be
fought again. When He returned to glory, as pictured in Psalm
24:7-10, the Lord of Hosts, who was crucified, was acclaimed as
"The Lord strong and mighty, the Lord mighty in battle." All
Heaven knew the forces He had vanquished; all the dwellers in
glory knew the meaning of the victory He had won. It was
jubilee in Heaven when Jesus went back again.

David and Goliath's unequal battle—the shepherd lad without a sword or spear meeting the mighty giant of the Philistines
striding proudly with his spear and sword and shield to mortal
combat in the valley of Elah—is one of the striking pictures in
the Old Testament of Golgotha.

David was misjudged by his brethren. Eliab, his eldest brother, said in anger, "Why camest thou down hither? and with
whom hast thou left those few sheep in the wilderness? I know
thy pride and the naughtiness of thine heart; for thou art come
down that thou mightest see the battle" (1 Sam. 17:28). What
stinging sarcasm and evil surmising! How untrue the charge of
pride and idle curiosity! David was one of the noblest examples
of meekness and lowliness in the Scriptures.

"To see the battle"? There was no battle till David came.
There would have been no battle had he not come. David was
there because his father sent him. David was there because he
was needed there.

David despised Goliath. "Who is this uncircumcised
Philistine that he should defy the armies of the living God?" (1
Sam. 17:26). David was fired with zeal for the dishonor that was
done to the name of God. "Thou comest to me with a sword,
and with a spear, and with a shield; but I come to thee in the
name of the Lord of hosts, the God of the armies of Israel, whom
thou has defied" (1 Sam. 17:45).

See the courage and the confidence of David as he meets the
towering giant. "David hastened, and ran toward the army to
meet the Philistine" (1 Sam. 17:48). How soon it was all over!
Goliath, like Dagon his god, lay stretched out with his face upon
the earth. In the forehead of his pride, Goliath was pierced with

the stone from David's sling. Before th
scarcely get their breath, there was Dav
cass of the giant, swinging above his
pulled from Goliath's sheath. Tears of
an eye as David returned to the ranks ᴐ.
of the boasting enemy of God in his hand.

The record says suggestively, "But there was no sᴠ.
hand of David" (1 Sam. 17:50). God wanted David to be a ·ᴗ_
of Him who:

> *"By weakness and defeat, He won the mead and crown;*
> *Trod all His foes beneath His feet, by being trodden down;*
> *He hell in hell laid low; made sin, He sin o'erthrew;*
> *Bowed to the grave, destroyed it so, and death by dying slew."*

You cannot think of David "slaying his tens of thousands" at Ephes-Dammim, without thinking of David's greater Son spoiling Satan of his power, and sin of its victory, at Calvary.

Samson, the mighty deliverer of God's people, bound by his brethren (Jud. 15:13), delivered to the Gentile Philistines, who shouted against him, is another type of Christ our Lord. The Philistines thought they had Samson secure. But when the Philistines shouted with joy, "the Spirit of the Lord came mightily upon him" (v. 14). Those new cords that bound Samson had never been broken. The might of the Spirit of God made those cords like flax that had been burned in the fire. Samson was just as free as if he had never been bound at all. He arose in his strength and utterly discomforted all his enemies.

Samson took hold of the symbol of death and with the jawbone of an ass slew a thousand men. Thus should we mortify or make dead the deeds of our bodies. Our enemies are those lusts and sins that once led us captive. Our warfare is a spiritual warfare. "We wrestle not against flesh and blood, but against principalities, against powers, against the rulers of the darkness of this world, against spiritual wickedness in high places" (Eph. 6:12). "For the weapons of our warfare are not carnal, but mighty through God to the pulling down of strongholds; casting down imaginations, and every high thing that exalteth itself against the knowledge of God, and bringing into captivity every thought to the obedience of Christ" (2 Cor. 10:4-5). "Forasmuch

Christ hath suffered for us in the flesh, arm yourselves
se with the same mind: for he that hath suffered in the
hath ceased from sin" (1 Pet. 4:1).

The victory of Samson was victory for the people of God. The
victory of the death of Christ is victory for us to lay hold of, that
we might walk in triumph over sin, for sin shall not have
dominion over us, for we are not under the law but under grace
(Rom. 6:14).

Joseph, who was beloved of his father, was hated by his
brethren; he was sold to the Ishmaelites; he was numbered with
transgressors, when he suffered for righteousness sake. But
Joseph came up out of prison to be "ruler over all the land of
Egypt" (Gen. 41:43); and to be called "Zaphnath-paaneah" (the
saviour of the world). So here again, in Joseph, God tells the
secret of Christ, who was hated, sold, and made to suffer, that
He might save the lives of others by "a great deliverance" (Gen.
45:7).

When the turbulent sea was raging against the mariners in
the ship in Jonah's day, the prophet said, "Take me up, and cast
me forth into the sea; so shall the sea be calm unto you" (Jonah
1:12). Jonah went down to the "bottoms of the mountains" for
three days and three nights. Thus the prophet Jonah was a sub-
stitute for others. He went into the angry billows that the trembling mariners might be saved from being engulfed in their fury.
Our Lord said many years later, "For as Jonas was three days
and three nights in the whale's belly; so shall the Son of Man be
three days and three nights in the heart of the earth" (Mt. 12:40).

Loving obedience took Isaac, the son of his father's love, to
the altar of sacrifice. There the ram in all the might of its mature
strength was held and consumed to ashes on Mount Moriah
(Gen. 22:1-14). Abraham saw the day of Christ (Jn. 8:56) on that
occasion and was glad. The father of all who believe said, "The
name of this place is Jehovah-jireh" for here "in the mount of the
Lord it shall be seen" (Gen. 22:14). Again and again, the Spirit of
God gave portrayals of this eternally glorious achievement, the
death of our Lord Jesus Christ.

The brazen serpent which Moses lifted up in the wilderness
(Jn. 3:14) tells the same story. When the people were dying
everywhere with the venomous poison in their veins, the way of

God for their life and salvation was revealed by God to Moses: "Make thee a fiery serpent, and set it upon a pole: and it shall come to pass, that every one that is bitten, when he looketh upon it shall live" (Num. 21:8). Our Lord explained the meaning of this type to Nicodemus when He said, "As Moses lifted up the serpent in the wilderness, even so must the Son of Man be lifted up; that whosoever believeth in Him should not perish but have eternal life" (Jn. 3:14-15).

The lamb on Abel's altar was Christ at Calvary. The Passover lamb "roast with fire" (Ex. 12:9), whose sprinkled blood sheltered the firstborn in Egypt, is typically "Christ our passover sacrificed for us" (1 Cor. 5:7). The "burnt offering" that was "killed before the Lord" and utterly consumed "for a sweet savor" (Lev. 1:1-9)—whether a bullock "strong to labor," or a lamb patient to suffer, or a goat surefooted to walk on high places, or turtle doves or young pigeons, birds of the heavens— was the same blessed One giving Himself for us, a sacrifice and an offering to God for a sweet smelling savor (Eph. 5:2).

The peace offering of Leviticus 3 is Christ again, making "peace by the blood of His cross" (Col. 1:20). He has brought God and men together in perfect peace without sacrificing righteousness or offending truth. The sin offering and trespass offering of Leviticus 4 and 5 add further truth that the work of Christ meets the need of what I am and what I have done.

Everyone of the millions of sacrifices offered on Jewish altars gave the same testimony to Christ, the perfect offering; and to His work, the perfect sacrifice. The blood of bulls and goats never put away sin (Heb. 10:4). Those sacrifices only had value insofar as they pointed to Christ. He "offered one sacrifice for sin forever, (and) sat down on the right hand of God" (Heb. 10:12). His death "purged our sins" (Heb. 1:3); and "perfected forever them that are sanctified" (Heb. 10:14).

All the prophets give witness to Him. The Spirit of Christ in the prophets of old "testified beforehand the sufferings of Christ, and the glory that should follow" (1 Pet. 1:11). The "testimony of Jesus is the spirit of prophecy" (Rev. 19:10).

The despondent and hopeless disciples who sadly turned from Jerusalem where their Lord was crucified and took that downhearted journey to Emmaus had their hearts warmed by the conversation of a Stranger who joined them. They never dreamed who that supposed Stranger was. After they had breathed their grief and despair into His ear, He said to them, "O fools, and slow of heart to believe all that the prophets have spoken: ought not Christ to have suffered these things, and to enter into His glory? And beginning at Moses and all the prophets, He expounded unto them in all the Scriptures the things concerning Himself" (Lk. 24:25-27). The wonder is that devout persons could read the Old Testament so long and over-look this constantly repeated reference to the sufferings and death of Emmanuel.

Put the testimony of Moses in the Torah, Isaiah and Zechariah in the prophets, with the testimony of David in the Psalms—and every detail of the rejection, sufferings, and death of our Lord is told. The Spirit of God in the Scriptures had dwelt on this theme continuously for centuries of prophetic witness. It was sung day and night in the psalms at the temple. It was portrayed in the slaying of the sacrifices every day of the year, on special occasions scores of times in a day. The whole procedure was told again and again by the inspired prophets. The very feelings of the Sufferer were described. Whole psalms spoke beforehand the very words of the heart and lips of the Saviour at Calvary. It was all so clearly told that we wonder at the blindness of Israel in not knowing that they were fulfilling their own Scriptures when they did these things to Him. As Paul preached at Antioch, "For they that dwell at Jerusalem, and their rulers, because they knew Him not, nor yet the voices of the prophets which are read every Sabbath day, they have fulfilled them in condemning Him. And though they found no cause of death in Him, yet desired they Pilate that He should be slain. And when they had fulfilled *all that was written of Him*, they took Him down from the tree, and laid Him in a sepulcher. But God raised Him from the dead" (Acts 13:27-30).

Christ died for our sins, sins against God. They were sins against infinite Majesty, and thus were infinitely insulting and base. They were sins against infinite authority, and thus were infinitely rebellious and wicked. They were sins against infinite goodness and thus were infinitely ungrateful and mean.

Had only an angel been offended, an angel could have made

restitution. But when the Eternal God had been so defiantly sinned against, and so wickedly transgressed, only God Himself could honor Majesty, make amends to Justice and Government, and satisfy the desires of Goodness and Love. Only the infinite God could deal with sin against the Infinite, with the approval of unswerving righteousness and truth.

Yet it was man who sinned, and therefore man must make restitution. This problem had only one solution; the great God must become a man to be a kinsman Redeemer; and to be able at the same time to uphold all the requirements of God's throne while making restitution for iniquity. None but God could do it, and none but a man would be permitted by justice to take the responsibility of man who had transgressed. There was only One who could redeem; thank God that One was willing. There was One who "was with God;" and "who was God" (Jn. 1:1-2); He was "the only begotten of the Father" (Jn. 1:14). He alone knew the infinite wrong that sin had done. He alone knew the infinite character of every sin and all evil. The Son alone, who knew God perfectly, could know what it meant to sin against Him. He knew that there was no other but Himself able to meet the situation; to display justice and to make love known. All praise forever to His name, the One who alone was able, was also willing, and willing with delight. "Then said I, Lo, I come; in the volume of the book it is written of me, I *delight to do Thy will, O My God*" (Ps. 40:7-8).

No words are more glorious than these, "Christ came" (Rom. 9:5). "Christ both died, and rose, and revived" (Rom. 14:9). "Christ died for our sins according to the Scriptures" (1 Cor. 15:3). This is the grandest proclamation that ever has been made in human language. These stupendous facts will be the wonder of all holy intelligences forever. That the great God should become a man, should be charged with the dreadful sins of men, should take on Himself not merely the matter of the results of sins, but even those sins themselves. This is the foundation and the fullness of the gospel. "Christ died for our sins according to the Scriptures."

May His cross be our glory. May His precious blood be our confidence and joy. May His conscious presence be our most coveted possession. May His Word strengthen our faith, and may His coming again be our daily hope and expectation.

> *"Calvary, O Calvary! Mercy's vast unfathomed sea;*
> *Love, eternal love to me; Saviour, we adore Thee."*

The death of Christ was the great revelation of God. The work of the cross infinitely transcends even the whole work of creation. Calvary was the master stroke of victory, assuring defeat both final and forever to all the mighty projects of Satan and his kingdom of darkness. The blood of Christ brings peace to our souls, and it will eventually bring peace founded upon righteousness in heaven and on earth.

LOVE'S VICTORY

As fades the subtle mirage in the Arab's desert land,
To leave the heart-crushed pilgrim, in a hopeless sea of sand;
As a brightening and a quiet, 'mid the thunder's prolonged roar,
Fades and ends with blacker tempest, than had churned the sea before.

So did pass from every bosom, hope which made the children sing,
And the vision of the glory, at the coming of the King;
Passed that little rift of sunshine, in the gathering judgment clouds,
When the Saviour, meek and lowly, rode acclaimed by Zion's crowds.

Weep! ye keepers of the temple, who the Lord of Heaven refused;
Weep for coming retribution, who God's love and grace abused;
As the pilgrim on the desert, as the sailor on the sea,
Wept for bitter disappointment, in their death-doomed misery.

Hark! ye Satan-goaded elders, priests of proud Jerusalem,
Stifling children's glad Hosannas!, lest the Son of God should reign;
You have earned your condemnation, you have brought your judgment down,
Curse and hatred laid on Jesus! Thorns on Mercy for a crown!

Would you stop God's streams of mercy? Dam up all His flowing love?
Stay their coming freely to us, while Jehovah reigns above?
Fools! to think your hand had triumphed, when you bound Him to the tree,
Fastened up the door of Heaven, with the nails of Calvary!
Could you keep the Nile from Egypt? turn its waters whence they came?

90

Can your wisdom stop the showers, when the clouds distill in rain?
Crucify Him! Crucify Him! Ah, thou cruel Pharisee!
Pride and sin thy heart have blinded, grace shall reign in spite of thee.

Never was dispensed such bounty, as from hands by iron bound,
Never grace, as when the Saviour, neither love nor mercy found,
Wrath but broke the dam for mercy, brought its blessings from above,
Hate which pierced Immanuel's bosom made a way for boundless love.

Power and might may vaunt o'er weakness, praying in Gethsemane,
Give to Christ a mocking scepter, and a throne at Calvary,
Now He reigns in power and glory, in the Father's house above,
Then He reigned in dying patience, Prince of Peace, and Lord of Love.

We shall see the kingly glory, which His heavenly brow adorns,
But His heart enthralling honors, are the cross and crown of thorns,
Man of Sin! your Armageddon shall your doom and downfall see,
But no battle's like Golgotha, where love gained the victory.

—Reprinted from *Moody Monthly*

CHAPTER EIGHT

The Renown of His Burial

Our Lord Jesus was buried by two members of the Sanhedrin, Joseph of Arimathaea, "an honorable counselor" (Mk. 15:43), and Nicodemus, a Pharisee and "a ruler of the Jews" (Jn. 3:1). These two noblemen of highest reputation and social standing carried the body of our Lord into that "sepulcher which was hewn out of a rock" (Mk. 15:46).

The sepulcher where they laid His body was in a garden (Jn. 19:41), doubtless like all Oriental gardens, with a stone wall around it, and a door that could be closed to keep out prowling animals and, if necessary, unwelcome men and women.

The "rich man" (Mt. 27:57) who owned the sepulcher evidently owned the garden also. Indeed, the garden spot had been purchased, the wall built, and the garden planted with the object of making the tomb in the comparatively soft rock inside. The sepulcher would not have been private and safe outside the garden. This garden and grave were "in the place where he was crucified" (Jn. 19:41). Those who carried Him to the tomb did not have far to go, for "the sepulcher was near at hand" (v. 42).

That tomb was "a new tomb" (v. 60). It was just completed and had never been used.

Three questions come to mind in considering the tomb:

1. *Why did Joseph make a sepulcher there?* His home was at Arimathaea, twenty-five miles from Jerusalem. Why did he hew a sepulcher at Jerusalem instead of at Arimathaea? There had been a time when Jerusalem was Joseph's glory, as it had been the psalmist's when he sang: "Walk about Zion, and go around

about her: tell the towers thereof. Mark ye well her bulwarks, consider her palaces; that ye may tell it to the generation following" (Ps. 48:12-13). Or in verses 1-3 of the same psalm: "Great is the Lord, and greatly to be praised in the city of our God, in the mountain of His holiness. Beautiful for situation, the joy of the whole earth, is Mount Zion, on the sides of the north, the city of the great King. God is known in her palaces for a refuge."

But the great King came, first as a babe to Bethlehem, and then to Jerusalem, as Zechariah had foretold, "meek, and riding upon an ass, and upon a colt, the foal of an ass." When the King came, however, the rulers of Jerusalem hated Him and utterly rejected Him. Now Christ was Joseph's glory, and Jerusalem's utter apostasy had taken away Joseph's pride in that city in whose palaces the Son of God had found no refuge.

2. *Why did Joseph select the garden and hew the sepulcher outside the gate of the city?* There were other sepulchers in Jerusalem beside those of the kings (2 Chron. 21:20; 24:25). Joseph was a rich man; why did he not prepare a tomb inside the city rather than outside in the place of the unclean? Outside the gate was outside the camp; this was the place of the unholy. Did Joseph prepare this tomb for himself, or for someone he loved, in the place of the unclean?

3. *Why did Joseph choose such a place as "Malefactors' Hill" for his garden and tomb?* Would he want friends visiting his grave to hear the shrieks and groans of dying victims on Roman crosses? That was the place where the vilest of criminals were crucified and hastily buried—"Golgotha," the "place of a skull." Why did Joseph want a sepulcher there?

The answers may be found in answering another question: Whom did Joseph bury in his tomb? He buried there the body of his Lord. Had Joseph known that Christ was to be crucified there, it would be certain that he made the tomb for Him. But did Joseph know? That is the fundamental question.

Nicodemus knew that Christ would be lifted up in death. He learned *that* the first time he visited the Lord by night (Jn. 3:14). Nicodemus and Joseph were fellow members of the Sanhedrin. Nicodemus and Joseph were fellow disciples of Christ. What one knew, the other would have known. The incidents involving Joseph and Nicodemus can be explained in no other way than that together these two instructed disciples studied the law, the prophets, and the psalms. How could they do otherwise?

After the first meeting of Nicodemus with the Lord, this Old Testament scholar went home knowing that Jesus of Nazareth was the Son of God given, as found in Isaiah 9:6 (cf. Jn. 3:16). He knew that Jesus was the Christ, the Son of Man, of Psalm 80:17 (cf. Jn. 3:14); and he knew He was to die by crucifixion, to be the antitype of the serpent on the pole of Numbers 21:8-9 (cf. again Jn. 3:14). Thus Nicodemus knew that Jesus of Nazareth was the Christ, the key to the prophets, the psalms, and the law. What an incentive that must have been to him to study the Old Testament Scriptures! What light must have been thrown on his instructed mind, full of the knowledge of the letter of the law!

Then when Joseph became a disciple too, what discoveries he and Nicodemus must have made!

When Nicodemus said in the Sanhedrin, "Doth our law judge any man, before it hear him, and know what he doeth?" (Jn. 7:51), how strange if Nicodemus were content to hear Him just once! It would not be according to the nature and impulses of the children of God, if Joseph and Nicodemus were disciples of Christ without having sat at His feet. They likely communed with their Lord on several occasions. Their very souls would demand it. Would the Lord refrain from telling them the details of His crucifixion and death, as He told His other disciples? The fishermen of Galilee were not familiar with the Scriptures and so did not take in the words of His death and resurrection. But masters in Israel would. The sequel shows that they did.

Even apart from any other enlightenment from the Lord, these two intelligent and devout students of the Old Testament could have discovered in its pages all the facts of Christ's death. From Genesis 22:14, they could learn that it would be on Mount Moriah: "In the mount of the Lord it shall be seen." Calvary is on the northern end of Moriah, the portion of the mountain which extends beyond the northern wall of the city.

From Exodus 12:6, Joseph and Nicodemus could tell the day of the year and the hour of the day the Passover Lamb was to be slain. And from Daniel 9:24-26 they should have been able to calculate the year when Messiah would be cut off.

Thus Joseph, if he was interested, could surely know; and the details show that he did know.

Peter and John "mourned and wept" with the others when Christ was crucified. It took the resurrection of Christ to instill boldness into them. "Now when they saw the boldness of Peter and John they took knowledge of them, that they had been with Jesus" (Acts 4:13). Those elders of Jerusalem knew that nothing but company with a resurrected Christ could have effected this radical change in them. But Joseph was bold when Jesus was dead! "Joseph of Arimathaea went in *boldly* unto Pilate" (Mk. 15:43). To the eleven all seemed lost at that moment. Why was Joseph so bold?

Joseph calmly commenced to perform what severed every link between him and the Sanhedrin, the temple, Jerusalem, and the Jews. What put that sacrificing boldness into Joseph? There is only one answer: Joseph knew that thus it should be; his faith was confirmed. Joseph knew that the Scriptures had been fulfilled. Joseph had the brightest faith at the darkest moment. Joseph had the greatest courage when there seemed to be absolutely nothing to warrant it.

More than that, the provision of the linen and the spices showed that not only the cross, but the burial was expected. When Joseph went to Pilate at the ninth hour and returned with the centurion to Calvary, he had no time to buy linen; it was ready before. Nicodemus had no time to purchase and mix a hundred pounds of spices either; they too were all ready. The grave in the garden nearby had been hewn by Joseph as a labor of love, and it too was ready on time.

The Jews expected the bodies to remain on the crosses until the Sabbath unless their legs should be broken (Jn. 19:31), but Joseph and Nicodemus knew when Christ would die.

Thus God in heaven used the spontaneous love of two devoted disciples of Christ to carry out His Word and honor His Son in His death, after He had cried out, "It is finished!" (Jn. 19:30).

Joseph knew that spices were needed, but he bought only the linen. Nicodemus knew that linen was needed, but he bought and mixed only the spices. This shows that the two friends had conferred beforehand and each knew what the other would bring. It was love to Christ that moved them to do it. They came together at the right moment and did the honors due a king to the One who so well deserved them.

This is what Andrew Bonar wrote of Joseph and the burial of Christ:

> At the hour of His death, behold the providence of God! A rich man, one of the honorable and esteemed in Jerusalem, a member of the Sanhedrin, and a disciple, unexpectedly appears at Calvary. This was Joseph of Arimathaea, without exception the most singularly noble character introduced to us in the Gospels. This rich man had been driven into concealment by the plots formed against him by the Jews, on account of his defending Jesus in the Sanhedrin openly (Lk. 23:51). 'Being a disciple,' not 'secretly,' but 'secreted,' or forced to hide by reason of their plots. He was the very contrast to timid Nicodemus—bold and unreserved.
>
> Behold, then, this man suddenly returns to the city; and finding that all is over, he boldly seeks the body of Jesus, his beloved Master. And next, he and Nicodemus—two rich men, but the one all boldness, the other nervously timid—lay the body in its silent tomb.
>
> And where is the tomb? "In the place where He was crucified" (Jn. 19:41); that is, at the very spot where criminals were put to death, and where they used to be buried. Extraordinary as it may appear, this very spot was the spot where Joseph's new tomb was hewn out of a rock! The stony sides of the tomb—the new tomb—"the clean place," where Jesus was laid—were part of the malefactors' hill. His dead body is "with the rich man and with the wicked" in the hour of His death! His grave is the property of a rich man; and yet the rocks which form the partition between His tomb and that of the other Calvary malefactors are themselves part of Golgotha. Is there not here a fulfillment of Isaiah's words to the letter, and that in a way so unlikely that no eye could have foreseen it but His who foreordained the whole?

In keeping with Bonar's comments on the meaning of the word "secretly" in John 19:38, W. E. Vine in his *Expository Dictionary of New Testament Words* renders the word literally as "having been hidden."

The question might well be asked, If Joseph of Arimathaea

was in hiding for fear of the Jews, what was he afraid of? He was certainly not afraid of losing his official position in the Sanhedrin; for if he had not forfeited it already by his protest against the deeds of that group, he certainly did when he asked for the privilege of burying the body of Christ. If the members of the Sanhedrin had not put him out of his counselorship before the burial of Christ, they certainly would then.

If Joseph of Arimathaea was afraid of being put out of the synagogue and away from the temple services, why did he do so drastic a thing as to handle a dead body on the night of the Passover? He was a "chief man among his people" (Lev. 21:4); to deliberately "defile" himself on such a holy occasion for one who was not a near relative would be unpardonable in the eyes of the temple authorities. Especially so when that dead body was His who was so utterly condemned by the chief priest as a blasphemer. Joseph, by his deliberate act of honoring the body of the Lord Jesus in the plain sight of the elders of Israel, showed he was not afraid of what they might do to him in the synagogue or temple.

When Joseph went boldly to Pilate and to Calvary when he might have had the very worst to fear from the bitter Jews, he showed plainly that he was not afraid of losing position, riches, friends, reputation, or his life itself. All he could lose he deliberately sacrificed without hesitation for Christ when he buried Him.

What then was Joseph afraid of? Why did he hide away, till our Lord cried, "It is finished!" on the cross?

Was it not that Joseph was afraid of the Jews putting him in prison before he accomplished the work he was prepared to do—to give to the Son of God the burial of a king? He had prepared that tomb for his Lord, and he did not want the elders of Israel to frustrate his purpose. All the events that followed showed Joseph had no fear for himself whatever. What this devoted man did, with the fellowship of Nicodemus, was perhaps the most courageous and most costly act of love to Christ that was ever performed.

But where did Joseph hide? He could not have been far from Calvary, for he knew immediately when our Lord said, "Father, into Thy hands I commend My spirit," and bowed His head in death. Right away Joseph went to Pilate. He was ready and waiting for that moment. Where could Joseph be in hiding and yet know so minutely what was happening on the cross?

There was one place where Joseph could hide without danger of being found by the pious Jews at the Passover season, and that was in the sepulcher he had hewed in the rock, which tomb was in the walled garden that belonged to him. Four days before the Passover every sepulcher had to be whitewashed to let the Jews know just where they were so they could be carefully avoided. Defilement from tombs and dead bodies prohibited the faithful from eating the Passover. All Joseph had to do was to fulfill the temple requirements by whitewashing his sepulcher and no one would go near it.

It seems to me that the tomb in the garden was the only logical place for the linen clothes to be placed in readiness as soon as they were bought. Also the hundred pound weight of spices mixed and prepared by Nicodemus must have been there also. A hundred pounds is a heavy load for a very strong man to carry far. You carry a hundred pounds of potatoes for two city blocks and see how your back and bones will ache. No, Nicodemus did not carry that weight of spices far. The spices must have been somewhere near to the place where Christ was crucified. That tomb in the garden, "near to the place where He was crucified," was the logical place.

When Joseph went to Pilate to beg Christ's body, he did not have the linen on his arm. Pilate wondered whether He were already dead. Probably the Jews had just left, asking that the crucified might have their legs broken to hasten their death. Pilate would not believe Christ was dead till he called the centurion who had charge of the crucifixion. While the messenger went, and until the centurion came, Joseph stood with Pilate, waiting. When the centurion affirmed that Jesus of Nazareth was dead, that He had died at the ninth hour when the darkness lifted, then Pilate commanded the centurion to release the body to Joseph. Together Joseph and the centurion returned to Calvary. The linen, therefore, must have been somewhere near at hand, for Joseph and Nicodemus commenced immediately to take the body down.

For my part, I am convinced that behind that garden wall

these two noblemen saw and heard all that was said and done at Calvary without themselves being seen or heard.

What must have been the thoughts in the hearts of the Jews at Calvary, as they still sat down and watched Him there, to see the centurion come back from Pilate with one of the foremost Jewish leaders walking by his side? Why was Joseph of Arimathaea coming with the centurion? What was he going to do? All the leaders of Jerusalem would know him. Some of them knew that he was a disciple of the Nazarene. The atmosphere must have been tense with questioning.

Only a few minutes after Joseph left the centurion, he returned, bringing over his arm yards and yards of fine white linen. With Joseph came another who was well-known as a ruler and a Pharisee. It was Nicodemus, bearing on his back a burden of one hundred pounds of spices—myrrh and aloes. These men of the strictest sect of the Jews' religion—what were they going to do? Would they dare to touch a dead body on such a sacred day as this? Were these counselors of Jerusalem going to associate themselves with Jesus of Nazareth now that He was dead? The people did not have long to wonder.

Joseph laid down his linen and Nicodemus laid down his spices on the sward near the cross. Next, those two noblemen of unblemished reputation walked to the foot of the cross and looked up at Him who hung upon it.

As Nicodemus looked up, he may have repeated: "As Moses lifted up the serpent in the wilderness, even so must the Son of man be lifted up: that whosoever believeth in Him should not perish, but have eternal life. For God so loved the world, that He gave His only begotten Son, that whosoever believeth in Him should not perish, but have everlasting life" (Jn. 3:14-16).

Then when Joseph looked at the gaping side, riven by the soldier's spear while he was away talking to Pilate, he may have quoted: "Reproach hath broken My heart; and I am full of heaviness: and I looked for some to take pity, but there was none; and for comforters, but I found none. They gave Me also gall for My meat; and in My thirst they gave Me vinegar to drink" (Ps. 69:20, 21). And perhaps he added, "They shall look upon Me whom they have pierced" (Zech. 12:10).

Together, with tender hands they drew out the nails, and if

the limbs were bound, they loosed the cords to take the body down. Would they not have repeated: "For dogs have compassed Me: the assembly of the wicked have enclosed Me: they pierced My hands and My feet" (Ps. 22:16)?

The two faithful friends, in the sight of the Jewish authorities now silent in their helpless wrath, bore the sacred body to the linen lying upon the earth and laid it down to prepare it for burial. They would straighten the arms by the body, then looking upon that face as they took the crown of thorns from His brow, they would say together, "His visage was so marred more than any man, and His form more than the sons of men" (Isa. 52:14).

Again, as they looked and wept, they could have repeated: "But He was wounded for our transgressions, He was bruised for our iniquities: the chastisement of our peace was upon Him; and with His stripes we are healed. All we like sheep have gone astray; we have turned every one to his own way; and the Lord hath laid on Him the iniquity of us all" (Isa. 53:5-6).

What a gospel meeting that was! The Jews were silent, helpless and bitter; the Roman soldiers awe-stricken because of the earthquake and because of His dying cry which had made them admit, "Surely this man was the Son of God."

Why do I believe that Nicodemus and Joseph quoted these verses? Well, I know that they knew them. I know also that if we had been in their place, we would have quoted them.

All could see that what the two men were doing was a labor of love. The folds of the napkin were wrapped about His head while the spices were poured in. Then, beginning at the feet, the body was carefully and reverently wrapped by Joseph, while Nicodemus poured in the myrrh and aloes. The fragrance of that preparation must have pervaded the whole atmosphere. That was the most fragrant spot in the universe of God.

When the body was ready, the women, who for shame had been afar off, drew near, and followed as mourners to the tomb, and beheld where He was laid. As Joseph and Nicodemus bore the precious burden to the tomb they would say, "They made His grave with the wicked, but with the rich man was His tomb" (Isa 53:9; see *Jamieson, Fausset and Brown's* commentary).

Having placed the body in the rockhewn sepulcher, Joseph and Nicodemus rolled a great stone to the door and departed.

Where did they go? What happened to them there? We must wait until the judgment seat of Christ to hear the end of this, as of many other thrilling stories of devotedness to Christ.

This that Joseph and Nicodemus did was one of the first evidences of victory in the midst of seemingly overwhelming and irretrievable defeat. "So let all thine enemies be confounded, O Lord: but let them that love Thee be as the sun when he goeth forth in his might" (Jud. 5:31).

Is there an illustration of the burial of Christ in the Old Testament teaching concerning the offerings? "And the priest shall put on his linen garment, and his linen breeches shall he put upon his flesh, and take up the ashes which the fire hath consumed with the burnt offering on the altar, and he shall put them beside the altar. And he shall put off his garments, and put on other garments, and carry forth the ashes without the camp unto a clean place" (Lev. 6:10-11).

The solemn care of the ashes of the burnt offering tells the story of how precious the object was which they represented. The burnt offering was wholly burnt. It was all for God, a sweet savor to the Lord. The garments the priest wore when he took the ashes from the altar and placed them beside it were not the garments he wore when he took them from beside the altar and carried them outside the camp. There is here a suggestion of the end of one priesthood when the ashes were taken from the altar, and the commencement of a new priesthood when they were carried to a clean place outside the camp.

When Nicodemus and Joseph took the body of our Lord from the cross, they broke every tie that bound them to the temple and its service. Were they of the priestly family of Aaron or of the consecrated tribe of Levi, they violated every link with the old order at Jerusalem when they deliberately handled a dead body on the eve of the Passover. They lost every claim to the privileges or service of the temple; they had completely broken with the old order.

But when they carried that body to a clean place outside the camp they were priests of a new order. They were members of that royal priesthood that is a "chosen generation, a holy nation, a peculiar people," ordained to show forth the praises of Him who hath called us out of darkness into his marvelous light (1

Pet. 2:9). They were of that "spiritual house, a holy priesthood, to offer up spiritual sacrifices, acceptable to God by Jesus Christ" (1 Pet. 2:5).

Joseph and Nicodemus carried the ashes of the Burnt Offering to a clean place outside the camp. That Burnt Offering was Christ, who was in every word and deed, in every motive and desire, a sweet savor to the Lord. He came of His own voluntary will; He glorified God on earth and finished the work God gave Him to do.

Joseph and Nicodemus not only as new priests reverently carried and deposited the ashes of the Burnt Offering in that clean tomb, but when they came to the cross to do this honor for Christ, they went forth unto Him without the camp, bearing His reproach (Heb. 13:13). None other of the Lord's disciples had so much to lose as they, and they gladly sacrificed all they had. May devotion to Christ cause us also to go forth unto Him outside this world's approval and honors, bearing His reproach.

CHAPTER NINE

His Resurrection

The resurrection of our Lord Jesus Christ was attested by "many infallible proofs" (Acts 1:3). On one occasion He was seen by "over five hundred brethren at once" (1 Cor. 15:6). Peter included the other eleven apostles with him when he said, "This Jesus hath God raised up, whereof we all are witnesses" (Acts 2:32). Our Lord's disciples handled Him (Lk. 24:39), talked with Him (Acts 1:6-9), and "did eat and drink with Him after He rose from the dead" (Acts 10:41). This companying with the disciples after our Lord's resurrection was for "forty days" (Acts 1:3).

Others were raised from the dead, like Lazarus (Jn. 11:43-44), and the son of the widow of Nain (Lk. 7:11-16), and the twelve year old daughter of Jairus (Mk. 5:35-43); but these all rose to die again. The renown of our Lord's resurrection is that when He emerged from death He brought the "keys of hell and death" with Him (Rev. 1:18). He was a conqueror, not conquered. Our Lord took His life again in resurrection (Jn. 10:17-18). Resurrection was His own act by His own inherent power.

Our Lord will never die again, for death has "no more dominion over Him" (Rom. 6:9). He ever lives to make intercession for us (Heb. 7:25).

There is no resurrection like His. There is nothing so glorious as resurrection; but there are elements of glory in the resurrection of Christ that could not possibly belong to any other. His resurrection sealed Satan's doom (Heb. 2:14-15); His resurrection is the assurance of our justification and resurrection also (Eph. 2:5-6; Rom. 4:25); His resurrection is the one act of power that shall never cease to be felt in heaven, earth, and hell—among the redeemed for blessing, upon His enemies to bind them at His pleasure, and to subdue all things to Himself.

Let us look at some of the "infallible proofs," and hear the testimony of some of the many witnesses. Some have borne unconscious and reluctant witness; others, who loved Him, have borne testimony that eventually cost them their lives. The words and actions of all persons implicated in the death of Christ have in some way added testimony to the fact of His resurrection.

The "watch" of soldiers who were sent to guard the tomb of Christ was taken from that "whole band" (Mt. 27:27), who were called together to strip and dishonor His person. It was they who put on Him the "scarlet robe" and the "crown of thorns" (vv. 28-29). It was they who "mocked Him" saying, "Hail, King of the Jews" (v. 29). It was they who "spat upon Him, and took the reed and smote Him on the head" (v. 30).

Pilate's thinly-veiled disgust with the elders of the Jews who asked for soldiers to guard the tomb is evident in his answer, "Ye have a watch: go your way, make it as sure as ye can" (Mt. 27:65). God says of them, "So they went, and made the sepulcher sure, sealing the stone and setting a watch" (v. 66). This was that wonderful precaution that caused laughter and ridicule in heaven. "He that sitteth in the heavens shall laugh, the Lord shall have them in derision" (Ps. 2:4). Was God afraid of Roman soldiers? What did an angel He sent care for the seal of Rome? Were these the soldiers who with the centurion stood at Calvary when the heavens grew dark? Did they hear their commander confess, "Truly this was the Son of God"? They did see the darkness and the earthquake, and must with the centurion have "feared greatly" (Mt. 27:54).

Now these callous men are left at Golgotha with their weapons and armor as the darkness of another night is coming on; they are there to guard the tomb where lies the body of Him they had so cruelly mocked in Pilate's hall. All they have to fear, they are told, is frightened disciples who may come in the darkness to steal His body. These soldiers watched and waited. The seal on the stone would awe any earthly power; no man dared to break that seal. The swords and shields of Roman soldiers were ready to keep all intruders away. The soldiers might have slept, but they did not.

As the first day of the week is near the dawning, this is what happened: "And behold there was a great earthquake: for the angel of the Lord descended from heaven, and came and rolled back the stone from the door, and sat upon it. His countenance was like lightning, and his raiment white as snow: And for fear of him the keepers did shake, and became as dead men" (Mt. 28:2-4).

This was a sight those soldiers would never forget. That exalted countenance! That majestic greatness that sat on the stone! As soon as any strength returned to their helpless limbs the soldiers fled the tomb for the city. They dared not go to the governor lest they perish for the neglect of their duty so they "showed unto the chief priests all the things that were done" (Mt. 28:11). These were the priests who accused Christ of blasphemy. These were the same priests who seemed so anxious for the soldiers to frighten away the disciples of the Lord from stealing His body from the grave. What were their feelings now as they listened to the story of the soldiers' experience? They were not deceived now. The darkness, the earthquake, and now the indisputable evidence of resurrection, told the story of Israel's dreadful mistake in crucifying the Son of God. There stood the soldiers; they had not failed in keeping the disciples of Jesus of Nazareth from the sepulcher they guarded. It was not men, but an angel from heaven that had frightened them. Surely the priests would forgive them under the circumstances.

What would the soldiers think now, when they listened to the turn-about-face of the priests? Instead of fearing the stealing of Christ's body by His disciples, those same priests now bring out their money bags and hand out "large money" for the soldiers to say the disciples stole the body while they slept. Should this come to the governor's ears—and who could keep it from them?—they would spend more money to persuade him and to secure them (Mt. 28:14). Thus this "watch" of soldiers given by Pilate to the Jews at their request, hoping to hinder any attempt of the Lord's disciples from circulating a report of a spurious resurrection, became one of the most incontrovertible witnesses of Christ's actual rising from the dead.

The soldiers were certainly not prejudiced in favor of the

Jews. The report these guards gave to the elders of Jerusalem was as manifestly true, as the report those elders paid them to circulate was manifestly false. The investigating of the meaning of the broken seal and empty tomb did not commence with either the Jewish officials who demanded the securing of the tomb, or with the Roman governor who gave the soldiers to assure it. The matter started with the appearance of the frightened soldiers at the temple, telling of the glorious angel who rolled away the stone and sat upon it. The way they told their story to the Jews showed how intense was their consternation. There was no need to institute an inquiry into the truth of these words of the soldiers. The agitated fright of hardened, callous men needed no corroboration. The unquestioning silence of the Jewish elders showed how unhesitatingly they accepted the soldier's report of what had taken place.

Thus, the first persons to whom the "watch" testified of the emptying of the sepulcher and the breaking of the Roman seal were the priests and elders of the Jews. The testimony to these blinded, obstinate rulers of Jerusalem was convincing in the extreme. Whatever their blindness before, they certainly knew the truth now. They had called Christ a deceiver when they sealed the stone. This probably was the honest conception of their perverted and obstinate hearts concerning Him. They would not listen to Christ's words; they would not believe the testimony to His works; He gave no honor to their worthless religion and they utterly rejected and despised Him.

To them Christ's confession of being the Son of God was blasphemy; with blinded zeal for their traditions they condemned Him to death with a good conscience. What a commentary on the stubbornness of human superstition and religious bigotry! This report of the Roman soldiers was an alarming revelation to the priests. It was true and they knew it. What should they do now? To confess the truth would condemn them in all their previous opposition to Jesus of Nazareth. It would mean to confess He was true and that they sinned in sending Him to the cross.

It seems that they did not hesitate for a moment. They immediately added wicked lying opposition to their previous blinded zeal. Their eyes were open now. They thought Christ was a deceiver at Calvary; they knew that they themselves were deceivers now. Pride that refused to be humbled chose rather to descend to the basest lying and deception, than to admit the truth that now was so patent before them. It was not a few men who made this hasty decision. The soldiers first told their story to the priests; these priests told it to the elders, who counselled together before the lying story was put into the soldiers' mouths. The whole action was as deliberate as it was false. There was no excuse now.

"Some of the watch came into the city (some of them probably ran away to hide) and showed unto the chief priests all the things that were done. And when they were assembled with the elders, and had taken counsel, they gave large money to the soldiers, saying, Say ye, His disciples came by night, and stole Him away while we slept. And if this comes to the governor's ears, we will persuade him and secure you. So they took the money and did as they were taught" (Mt. 28:11-15).

This report of the soldiers to the chief priests, and then to the elders, must have been after the lapse of many hours. The rolling away of the stone occurred before the break of day. The Sanhedrin would not be in session until later in the morning. The soldiers had evidently considered the best course for them to pursue to preserve their lives, seeing they had apparently failed in their duty. They had committed a great crime in the Roman army—to fail to watch a sealed property. They were guilty of death, and doubtless wanted to escape the penalty.

The chief priests and elders of the Jews showed the soldiers how their lives could be saved. The priests who would not put the silver of Judas into the treasury did not hesitate to take "large money" out of the treasury to further their lying schemes. This is the propensity of human nature: very religious one day and very wicked the next. Refusing very sanctimoniously to put the price of blood into the treasury on Thursday, but taking the price of blood, of hypocrisy, and of deceit, out of the treasury on Sunday! What loathsome wickedness for religious leaders!

The soldiers took the money and did as they were taught. They circulated in Jerusalem the story that they were all sound asleep when the disciples of the Lord came and stole His body.

Pilate was disgusted when he gave the Jews the watch of soldiers to keep the disciples of the Lord from stealing His body from the tomb. Pilate's own conscience told him Jesus was a just person. The supernatural darkness must have greatly increased Pilate's fears. At the trial he feared when he heard that Jesus said He was the Son of God; he was afraid that it might be true. Pilate knew that for envy the Jews had delivered Christ to him. His wife warned him to have nothing to do with that "just person," because of what she had suffered in a dream because of Him. The testimony of Joseph of Arimathaea when he went to Pilate to beg Christ's body must have deepened these impressions. Who knows what Pilate asked Joseph, or what that honored counselor told the Roman governor? The unexpected fact of so honored a gentleman as Joseph coming so boldly to beg for the body could not help but raise the curiosity of Pilate to know why he should brave the wrath of the Jews to give an honored burial to Him whom the nation so utterly rejected. Joseph probably told Pilate what Jesus Christ was to him. And the centurion who came to tell Pilate of Christ's actual death was the one who had said, "Truly this man was the Son of God."

After all this testimony, when Pilate heard from the lips of the priests that Jesus said He would rise again, there is every reason to think Pilate would fear this is what might actually take place. And when the soldiers' story came to Pilate's ears, would he believe it? He was too astute a man for that. Pilate would not believe a story so contrary to human reason. When the soldiers had to appear before him he would say, "What! All you men asleep at one time? All of you so sound asleep that you did not waken when the grave by which you were sleeping was broken into? If you were so sound asleep, how did you know what happened?" Those soldiers could not keep the truth from Pilate. He would get it out of them. What would Pilate do then? Hardened sinner though he was, he was not guilty of such hypocrisy and deceit. I doubt very much whether the money of the priests saved the lives of the soldiers.

All these happenings must have impressed the soul of Pilate with the fact of our Lord's resurrection. It was a remarkable testimony to him. When Pilate was governor in Jerusalem, how could he be ignorant of the testimony that was so publicly given there of the resurrection of our Lord? Had the story of the sleeping soldiers not reached Pilate's ears from others, I could not understand him not investigating the soldiers whom he placed at the tomb, to hear from their lips what actually happened.

All Jerusalem was stirred about Christ. Pilate had reason to be as deeply concerned as anyone. His natural superstition and curiosity would impel the governor to discover the sequel to the condemnation, death, and reputed resurrection of Jesus of Nazareth. Being so deeply involved, how could Pilate rest, knowing only half the truth? There is scarcely a possibility that those soldiers did not stand before their supreme ruler and master in Palestine, to tell him all they knew of the disappearance of the body of Christ from the grave.

Did the priests come to Pilate, as they promised, to bribe him to let the soldiers go? They were heartless enough to let the soldiers die if that suited their purpose. The soldiers would certainly tell Pilate all the truth before they were slain with the sword. Suppose the priests did come with their money to Pilate, what would he say to them? "You contemptible hypocrites, you know the soldiers were not sleeping; you know what happened; and now you want to silence the truth by such a story as this!" Unless the sight of the money would silence the lips of Pilate, words such as these would sting the ears of the priests.

Pilate was one man in Jerusalem who must have known that Jesus Christ rose from the dead. The soldiers who watched the grave and saw the heavenly visitor, and then took the hush money from the priests of the temple must also have known the truth. Whether either Pilate or the soldiers ever humbled themselves before God in confession is another matter. Some tradition says that Pilate was converted. If it were so, it was a marvel of the grace of God. If any of the soldiers were saved, it was in answer to His intercession who prayed, "Father, forgive them, for they know not what they do" (Lk. 23:34).

If the elders of Jerusalem believed their own story of the disciples breaking the Roman seal and stealing Christ's body, why did they not bring those disciples before the judgment seat to answer to this charge? When Peter and John witnessed so fearlessly before all the assembled rulers of Jerusalem of the resurrection of Christ (Acts 4:5-6), why did no one say a word regarding those disciples taking the body from the grave? Their silence in that matter should have convinced the listening people that the story was not true. The priests should have said to Peter and John, "Raised from the dead? Nonsense! You disciples stole the body from the grave when the soldiers were asleep." No such charge was made. No such words were spoken. No member of the Sanhedrin had the temerity to make such a foolish charge in such a congregation, and in the face of the testified facts.

The resurrection of Christ needs no confirmation from circumstantial evidence. The evidences are there, and they are impossible to refute. The Jews to this day repeat the ridiculous story of the disciples stealing His body from a sealed tomb while a whole watch of soldiers were sound asleep. They all know that the sleeping soldiers were the first to broadcast the story. No sane person should receive such testimony.

But there was also external evidence of the most convincing sort. These recorded miracles of the death and resurrection of Christ are united in one story. There was the darkness over all the land for three hours (Mt. 27:45); there was the rending of the veil of the temple from the top to the bottom (Mt. 27:51); and there was the appearance of the dead in Jerusalem from the opened graves after His resurrection (Mt. 27:52-53). A second earthquake is said to have occurred when the angel rolled the stone from the grave (Mt. 28:2).

Not only were these incidents witnessed to by the disciples immediately, the account of them was written in the Gospel according to Matthew not more than seven years after they happened This Gospel was circulated and read for thirty years at Jerusalem before the destruction of the city and temple.

Had this writing not been true, would such matters of common experience have been declared? What a blow to Christianity it would have been to write about a three hours' darkness over all Palestine if it did not take place! How could disciples of Christ witness to earthquakes that no one knew anything about? Those incidents were too recent and too generally known to be refuted. None of the enemies of the Lord at that time disputed the fact of these things. Would they not have done so had they not been true?

Christ and Christianity were not popular in the land, nor among the people where the gospel had its beginning. Christianity was not carried along by popular acclaim,

Christianity had to face the opposition of prejudice and bigotry in the very city where Christ was crucified and where He rose from the dead.

When the priests of the temple were such implacable enemies of the gospel of Christ, if the veil of the temple was not rent from the top to the bottom, do you think those priests would not have borne united testimony to this lie? What stronger case could they have brought against the genuineness of the gospel of Matthew than by declaring the record of the rending of the veil to be a lie? When no mention of the rending of the veil being false was made by any of the priests of the temple in their bitter discussions with the Lord's disciples, all must know that this testimony was true.

To perform the ministrations of the temple, the veil had to be sewed up again, then the place of the rent would certainly show. The first Gospel to be written and circulated, containing the account of the rending of the veil of the temple, proves that witness to be true. No Jew ever denied it in the days of the Acts.

If the veil were rent, none but God could do it. It was a miracle for God to do it without tearing the temple apart. The veil was not fastened securely to the walls of the building that spread apart, and so rent. The veil was hung freely from the top, and only fastened there. An invisible hand took hold of the veil at the top and tore it with terrific force to the bottom. That hand was the hand of God. Why did He do it then, except as a testimony for Christ, and against the priests, who in blind zeal for those outward things nailed the Son of God to Calvary? It was what Christ said about the temple that brought upon Him the rage of the priests. In rending the veil God witnessed to His Son, and against them.

The deep-seated prejudice that, after finding the veil rent by the hand of God, proceeded to bribe the soldiers to circulate a lie to hide the testimony to our Lord's resurrection, was the evidence of enmity and hatred that refused to be convinced or enlightened. When the priests of Jerusalem took these steps of blindness and opposition to Christ, there was absolutely no hope for the nation. God had spoken, but they refused to listen. He whom God sent from heaven, they utterly hated. Pride compassed them as a chain, binding them hand and foot, through the dogged perversion of their will. They would not come to Christ that they might have life. Now they would not believe that they might be saved. In fact, Paul suggests that they took a veil and covered their minds that the truth might not shine in (see 2 Cor. 3:14).

Think with me about the linen clothes. Here is the testimony of Scripture: "Then took they the body of Jesus, and wound it in linen clothes with the spices, as the manner of the Jews is to bury" (Jn. 19:40). "Peter therefore went forth and that other disciple, and came to the sepulcher...The other disciple did outrun Peter, and came first to the sepulcher. And he stooping down, and looking in, saw the linen clothes lying...and the napkin that was about His head, not lying with the linen clothes, but wrapped together in a place by itself. Then went in also that other disciple, which came first to the sepulcher, and he saw and believed. For as yet they knew not the scripture, that He must rise again from the dead. Then the disciples went away again unto their own home" (Jn. 20:3-10).

The seemingly unimportant detail of the linen clothes, that wrapped the body of our Lord, being left in the tomb, though unnoticed by the women, was a convincing proof of resurrection to both Peter and John. It was not merely the fact that the linen was there, although that was a matter to arrest attention; but the place of the linen of the body, separated from the napkin of the head, and the way the linen was wrapped together—these forced on the observant disciples the conviction of their Lord's resurrection.

Had the body of Christ been carried from the grave, linen clothes would have gone with Him. There would have been neither time nor purpose to remove the wrappings of the body.

However, had the hand of man removed the linen from both body and head, all would have been thrown on a heap in the grave. But here lay the linen of the body where the body had been, and the linen of the napkin where the head had been. Not only were the parts separated, but the linen was "wrapped together." Just as the hands of Joseph and Nicodemus had wrapped the folds of white linen around the body of their Lord, there they were still. Without disorder, the linen that formed the napkin around His head, was still there, folded as those loved ones had left it when they placed Him in the sepulcher. No human hand could have folded the linen so, without a body to wrap the bands around. No one but the women had been to the sepulcher, and certainly no one had had time to fix the clothes of burial in this peculiar fashion. What purpose would any person have had to attempt to wrap the linen in this way even had it been possible?

Those linen clothes were a miracle. Both Peter and John knew without a doubt what they meant. The body that was wrapped in those garments had disappeared from them without disturbing them any more than a spirit would have done. Resurrection had taken place. Although Peter and John did not yet know the scripture that He must rise again, those linen clothes convinced them absolutely that their Lord rose from the tomb.

It is these simple details, so artlessly told, that convince the thoughtful reader of the truth of the story. Who would have imagined such a peculiar detail as linen clothes left undisturbed in the tomb? No concocted story would have introduced anything so unlikely, or so unusual. This is not in the province of imagination, as any balanced judgment must admit. Hallucination might account for some erratic imaginations, but not for an account of undisturbed burial garments in the grave. When our Lord left behind Him in the tomb the fragrant linen that love and honor bound to Him for burial, He showed how completely resurrection left the former condition of His humiliation behind.

When our Lord comes, we too shall receive a body of glory like His body; then, all the evidences of our weakness will be forever left behind. "It doth not yet appear what we shall be, but we know that when He shall appear we shall be like Him for we shall see Him as He is" (1 Jn. 3:2).

> *The Lord is risen; with Him we also rose,*
> *And in His grave see all our vanquished foes;*
> *The Lord is risen: beyond the judgment land,*
> *In Him, in resurrection life, we stand.*
>
> *The Lord is risen: the Lord is gone before,*
> *We long to see Him, and to sin no more!*

115

The Lord is risen: our trumpet shout shall be,
"Thou hast prevailed! Thy people, Lord, are free!

Another major piece of clear evidence for the resurrection is the conversion of Saul of Tarsus. Luke, the beloved physician, tells the whole story in the ninth chapter of his inspired book of the Acts. Threatenings and slaughter against the disciples of the Lord were so completely occupying the thoughts of the persecutor, Saul, that the breath he breathed was saturated with this unmitigated enmity. He was "breathing out threatenings and slaughter against the disciples of the Lord" (Acts 9:1). This was the blinded zealot who was smitten to the earth when nearing Damascus. "Saul, Saul, why persecutest thou Me?" the Lord asked from heaven.

"Who art thou Lord? And the Lord said, I am Jesus whom thou persecutest: it is hard for thee to kick against the pricks" (Acts 9:4-5). "And he trembling and astonished said, Lord, what wilt Thou have me to do?" (v. 6). "And Ananias went his way, and entered into the house; and putting his hands on him said, Brother Saul, the Lord, even Jesus, that appeared unto thee in the way as thou camest, hath sent me, that thou mightest receive thy sight, and be filled with the Holy Ghost. And immediately there fell from his eyes as it had been scales: and he received sight forthwith, and arose, and was baptized. Then was Saul certain days with the disciples which were at Damascus" (vv. 17-19). "But Saul increased the more in strength, and confounded the Jews which dwelt at Damascus, proving that this is very Christ" (v. 22).

This conversion to Christ has been told by Saul again and again. Standing on the stairs of the castle adjoining the temple in Jerusalem, after being mercilessly beaten and almost torn to pieces by the infuriated Jews, Saul made his defense and told the story of his conversion to the Lord Jesus. The substance of this stirring address is found in Acts 22:1-21. Nothing but truth could account for this Hebrew of the Hebrews telling the story of the revelation of Christ to his soul. Saul had been just as mad as his accusers were this day, and for the very same reason. Grace to Gentiles! A Saviour for Gentile dogs! "Away with such a fellow from the earth!" (Acts 22:22).

In Acts 26, Paul the apostle tells the same facts to King Agrippa and to the company assembled with him. He ended by confessing, "Having therefore obtained help from God, I continue unto this day, witnessing to both small and great, saying none other things than those which the prophets and Moses did say should come: that Christ should suffer, and that He should be the first that should rise from the dead, and should show light unto the people and to the Gentiles" (Acts 26:22-23).

What Paul had already suffered, what his present testimony exposed him to in the presence of his bitter brethren, show plainly that Paul knew the truth of what he testified, that Jesus was the Christ, and that He rose from the dead and that he himself had been with Him. No vision or dream would give such indomitable strength to witness and to suffer. No philosophical reasoning would so powerfully have impressed his hearers. The Living, Resurrected Christ was the one all-absorbing reality to Paul the apostle, who was before, the blaspheming Pharisee, Saul of Tarsus, perhaps the most violently bitter enemy Jesus Christ ever had.

Saul of Tarsus was in Jerusalem during the eventful days of the death and resurrection of Christ. He tells us himself that he was brought up in Jerusalem "at the feet of Gamaliel" (Acts 22:3). This Gamaliel was said to be "a Pharisee, a doctor of the law, had in reputation among all the people" (Acts 5:34).

Gamaliel must have had authority in the council, for when the rest took counsel to slay the apostles for their testimony to the resurrection of Christ, he "commanded to put the apostles forth a little space" (Acts 5:34). So many things had happened since the council in which Gamaliel sat had delivered Jesus to Pontius Pilate, that this doctor of the law was determined that now the Sanhedrin must proceed with caution. But however slow and cautious the master, Gamaliel, might be in persecuting the witnesses of Christ, his student, Saul of Tarsus, was most rabid in accomplishing whenever he had the opportunity. When the apostles were in the hands of Gamaliel he commanded that instead of putting them to death, they should wait and see whether or not this work were of God. But Saul of Tarsus said of himself, "I persecuted this way unto the death, binding and delivering into prisons both men and women" (Acts 22:4).

The testimony of Nicodemus and Joseph of Arimathaea had been entirely lost on Saul of Tarsus. What Saul thought of the supernatural darkness during the last sufferings of Christ and of the earthquake at the ninth hour we do not know. Neither the foolish story of the soldiers at the grave of Christ nor the unflinching testimony of Stephen and other Christians seemed to make the slightest impression on Saul. He was still "breathing out threatenings and slaughter against the disciples of the Lord" (Acts 9:1). There never had been a more striking example of persistent bigotry and blinded zeal for traditional superstition than was seen in the early days of Christianity in Saul of Tarsus, the Pharisee. Saul was exceedingly zealous of the traditions of his fathers, and exceedingly mad against the Christians.

Did Saul believe in the actual resurrection of Christ? Of course he did not. The soul of Saul rebelled against even listening for one moment to any testimony concerning what was to him so hated an impossibility. He shut his eyes to Stephen's radiant countenance and his ears to Stephen's forceful words, holding the garments of those who wanted their arms free to cast the stones that crushed the life out of the first martyr of the church. The zeal of Saul was both deaf and blind, but it was sincere and full of energy because of the perverted teachings of his tutors. Saul was not a hypocrite. Saul could crush to death helpless men and women with a good conscience; he imagined he was serving God when he was tormenting those who were the true children of the Almighty.

The conversion of Saul of Tarsus is one of the stumbling blocks of unbelief. Infidels think there are things in the Bible that are stumbling blocks to faith. Those who know the Bible best have never found these stones of stumbling in its pages. When unbelief blindly walks its obstinate way, if it allows itself to run into the facts of the conversion of Saul of Tarsus, I cannot understand how it can dispose of this obstacle to unbelief. What explanation could atheism give to the remarkable change in such a remarkable person as Saul of Tarsus, from violent and conscientious opposition to the gospel of Christ, to a lifelong self-denying and self-sacrificing devotion to that same gospel? What worked this change? What made Paul the apostle out of Saul the persecuting Pharisee? Paul himself says it was the fact of

Christ's resurrection. Saul of Tarsus met Christ on the Damascus road. Jesus of Nazareth in resurrection spoke to Saul in such a way that there was no possibility of mistaking either the Person or the message. The evidence was overwhelming.

The apostle Paul refers to the resurrection of Christ in each of the epistles he wrote to the churches. That resurrection was a great fundamental fact to Paul. It had a most prominent place in all his witnessing in the synagogues of the Jews. To Paul the resurrection of Christ confirmed, as the seal of God, the Deity of the Lord's person and the fact of His miraculous works.

The first epistle written by Paul was to the newly saved Gentile church of the Thessalonians. The last epistle this veteran evangelist wrote was to his fellow-laborer and son in the faith, Timothy. In both these letters Paul makes prominent mention of the resurrection of Christ. A raised and living Christ at God's right hand was Paul's thrilling confidence when he commenced his preaching in Damascus and Thessalonica, and the same glorious fact filled his soul when he knew his course was run.

This is what Paul wrote to the church of the Thessalonians so shortly after their conversion: "Ye turned to God from idols, to serve the living and true God; and to wait for His Son from heaven, *whom He raised from the dead,* even Jesus which delivered us from the wrath to come" (1 Thess. 1:9-10).

This is what he wrote to Timothy from his prison in Rome when his work and warfare were done: "Remember that Jesus Christ of the seed of David, *was raised from the dead* according to my gospel" (2 Tim. 2:8).

When Paul gave the church at Rome, by the Spirit's inspiration, that masterly treatise on the gospel which we call, "The Epistle to the Romans," he commenced by telling us that "the gospel of God" was "concerning his Son Jesus Christ our Lord, which was made of the seed of David according to the flesh; and declared to be the Son of God with power, according to the Spirit of holiness, by *the resurrection from the dead*" (Rom. 1:3-4).

In this same epistle we are told that the resurrection of Christ was for our justification (Rom. 4:25); the resurrection of Christ has, for the believer, ended the dominion of sin (Rom. 6:4-14); we are married to Him who was raised from the dead to bring forth fruit unto God (Rom. 7:4); and He who was raised from the dead makes intercession for us in heaven, so that we shall never be separated from the love of Christ (Rom. 8:34-39).

In the epistle to the Corinthians we have that imperishable fifteenth chapter on the resurrection of Christ and of His people. The facts adduced could not be refuted then, and they cannot be refuted today. When that declaration was written, the greater part of five hundred witnesses were still alive. These were men and women who had seen Christ, talked with Him, and even touched Him, these appearances occurring over a period of forty days. With the greatest emphasis possible, Paul wrote, "Now is Christ risen from the dead, and become the firstfruits of them that slept" (v. 20).

When the Galatians were being corrupted from the sincerity of the gospel by law-keepers, Paul commenced his faithful epistle to them by giving a statement of his apostleship and authority from God. He wrote: "Paul an apostle, (not of men, neither by man, but by Jesus Christ and God the Father, who raised Him from the dead")" (Gal. 1:1).

A more marvelous unfolding of the power of Christ's resurrection, both in Him and in us, could not be found than that in the first chapter of Ephesians. That declaration of the exceeding greatness of God's power will be seen in heaven forever. It was far more stupendous than the work of creation.

There are references to the resurrection of Christ in the epistles to the Colossians and to the Philippians that might well exercise our hearts. To the Colossians, Paul wrote: "If ye then be risen with Christ, seek those things which are above, where Christ sitteth on the right hand of God. Set your affections on things above, not on things on the earth" (Col. 3:1-2).

In his letter to the Philippians, Paul writes his own ambition in these stirring words: "That I may know Him, and the power of His resurrection, and the fellowship of His sufferings, being made conformable unto His death" (Phil. 3:10).

Everything that Saul of Tarsus as a zealous Jew would have died for, he counted but refuse for Christ. The soul of Saul had once burned with a zeal for the traditions of his fathers. When he considered that Jesus of Nazareth and His disciples were contrary to these traditions, he was "exceedingly mad against them." Before he was saved, he would not allow himself to consider for one moment any testimony to the resurrection of Christ. No witness of men or of miracle had the slightest weight with him. It seemed that after Stephen's death, nothing whatever could penetrate the armor of blinded bigotry with which he was encompassed. Saul of Tarsus was as great an enemy to Christ as ever breathed. When God by His miracles and signs, with the testimony of His servants, goaded Saul, as a master would a stubborn ox, then Saul kicked against the pricks. Nothing reached his perverted conscience until the Lord Himself appeared to Saul and spoke to him with a voice that could not be mistaken. He answered, "Who art Thou, Lord?" What a question for a praying Pharisee! What a confession for an "Hebrew of the Hebrews!"

That sight of Christ in resurrection, that revelation of Jesus of Nazareth in the excellent glory, that declaration that Jesus was Jehovah, turned the world of Saul of Tarsus completely upside down. Such a perfect reversal of all that made up a bigot's life had seldom been seen. Inside and out, Saul of Tarsus was now the very opposite of all that he had been before. The resurrection of Christ that he had rejected with all the bitter hatred of his passionate soul, now he accepted with a repentance and devotion that was as deep as his flaming opposition had been before.

Who could account for this radical and complete change in a man like Saul of Tarsus apart from the confession that what Saul said of himself was true? Who could find a reason to explain the fact of the adherence of Paul to his confession of Christ's resurrection, in the face of a whole life of loss, and shame, and suffering, and isolation, and death, for that testimony, without the acknowledgement that the astute and honest Paul knew that Christ's resurrection was a reality?

Paul's inspired testimony and undaunted life are proofs of the fact of Christ's resurrection from the dead. Men like Lord Lyttleton and Gilbert West with giant intellects but honest hearts have faced the problem of the conversion of Saul of Tarsus and, losing their infidelity as Saul did his blind religion at the feet of Christ, have risen to proclaim that Jesus who was crucified rose again the third day and is Lord. Millions have done what Paul by the Spirit says every man should do. I stop with Paul's imperishable testimony: "That if thou shalt confess with thy mouth the Lord Jesus, and shalt believe in thine heart that God hath raised Him from the dead, thou shalt be saved" (Rom. 10:9).

The promise of His resurrection was made very clear in the Scriptures. Notice the following: "And we declare unto you glad tidings, how that *the promise* which was made unto the fathers, God hath fulfilled the same unto us their children, in that *He hath raised up Jesus again;* as it is written in the second psalm, Thou art My Son, this day have I begotten Thee" (Acts 13:32-33).

This fact that the resurrection of Christ was promised in the Old Testament scriptures is one of the unanswerable proofs of this foundation truth of our salvation. Peter and Paul in their early recorded testimony quoted at least four places in the Psalms and one in Isaiah where the resurrection of Christ was foretold. These references tell the story of why Christ rose again.

Peter in Acts 2:25-28 quotes from Psalm 16:8-11: "For David speaketh concerning Him, I foresaw the Lord always before my face, for He is at my right hand, that I should not be moved: Therefore did my heart rejoice, and my tongue was glad; more-over also my flesh shall rest in hope: because Thou wilt not leave my soul in hell, neither wilt Thou suffer Thine Holy One to see corruption. Thou hast made known to me the ways of life; Thou shalt make me full of joy with Thy countenance."

Peter also commented upon this question as follows: "Men and brethren, let me freely speak unto you of the patriarch David, that he is both dead and buried, and his sepulcher is with us unto this day. Therefore being a prophet, and knowing that God had sworn with an oath to him, that of the fruit of his loins, according to the flesh, he would raise up Christ to sit on his throne; he seeing this before spake of the resurrection of Christ, that his soul was not left in hell, neither his flesh did see corruption. This Jesus hath God raised up; whereof we all are witnesses. Therefore being by the right hand of God exalted, and having received of the Father the promise of the Holy Ghost, he hath shed forth this, which ye now see and hear. For David is not ascended into the heavens; but he saith himself, The Lord said unto my Lord, Sit thou on My right hand, until I make Thy foes Thy footstool. Therefore let all the house of Israel know assuredly, that God hath made that same Jesus, whom ye have crucified, both Lord and Christ" (Acts 2:29-36).

Here Peter shows that David could not have been speaking of himself; but was most assuredly speaking of Christ who in death saw no corruption. None other but Jesus of Nazareth has died without seeing corruption. The words of Psalm 16 can be explained in no other way than by applying them to Christ, whose soul was not left in hell, nor did His body see corruption.

The dying Saviour who passed through death, speaks in Psalm 16:11 and says, "Thou wilt show me *the path of life.*" The great achievement of the Christ of Psalm 16 is this opening of the Path of Life. He went down into the depths of death, but He came up again. He entered Satan's stronghold, but He could not be imprisoned there. He was held on the cross by His love, but He could not be holden of the cords of death.

The path of life was through death. The path of life is the path of resurrection. Death is no longer "straitly shut up" like Jericho. Since our Lord died and rose again, there is a way from death into life. He is the Captain of our salvation; He overcame every enemy; He "spoiled principalities and powers." Now the path of life to His people is the path of faith. There is a way from death to life simply by believing on His name.

"Verily, verily, I say unto you, he that heareth My word, and believeth on Him that sent Me, hath everlasting life, and shall not come into condemnation; but is passed *from death unto life*" (Jn. 5:24).

Peter quoted from Psalm 110 where our Lord is acclaimed as a Priest forever after the order of Melchizedek. This psalm commences with a prophecy of resurrection. These are the words of Peter as he witnessed in Jerusalem: "For David is not ascended into the heavens, but he saith himself, The Lord said unto my Lord, Sit Thou at my right hand, until I make Thy foes Thy footstool" (Acts 2:34-35; compare Ps. 110:1).

The first words of Psalm 110 were quoted by our Lord to the Pharisees when He asked them this question, "What think ye of Christ? whose Son is He?" (Mt. 22:42); they answered immediately, "The Son of David." Then Christ asked them this question, "How then doth David in spirit call him Lord, saying, The Lord said unto my Lord, sit Thou on My right hand, until I make Thy foes Thy footstool?" No man then was able to answer Him a word. The scriptures they treasured and trusted in revealed that the Messiah would be the Lord.

This verse that proves Jesus to be the Lord implies His resurrection. It was when He was raised from the dead that He was bidden to sit at God's right hand. The honored title *Lord* was given to Him then by God.

This precious psalm that looks at Christ the Lord in heaven at God's right hand says of Him, "Thou art a *priest forever* after the order of Melchizedek" (Ps. 110:4). Here is a further blessed truth associated with the resurrection of Christ, *His eternal priesthood*. Not only did He come out of death to blaze the path of life for us, He ever lives at God's right hand for us, to be the needed High Priest of His people. The life He gives is eternal life. It is life in its fullness when we receive it. It is life that obtains its perpetual freshness and power from Him who sits for us in heaven. He is the Captain of our Salvation bringing us there, and for us He sits an eternal Priest on the throne.

Since our imperfections are so many, what a blessing to have a perfect High Priest to represent us! If we cannot trust our own faithfulness, we surely can trust His. If we cannot save ourselves to the uttermost because of our utter helplessness, He who ever lives to make intercession for us is most perfectly able (see Heb. 7:25). That is the very reason He rose again. That is the very reason He is on the throne of God. We needed a Priest who was God as well as man. God to be majestically able, and man to be sympathetically willing. This is Christ Jesus our Lord in resurrection.

In Acts 4:10-11 Peter charges the Jews with the death of Him whom God raised from the dead, saying: "This is the stone which was set at nought of you builders, which is become the head of the corner." This quotation is from Psalm 118:22. Here then is another blessed fact of Christ's resurrection; He is *the stone* "set at nought" by Israel's builders, whom God has made the absolutely necessary *"head of the corner."*

God has a building, and Christ is the foundation (Isa. 28:16) upon which it rests. Christ is also the *"precious corner stone"* making the wall beautiful and holding the building together (Isa. 28:16). The Lord Jesus is also the *"headstone"* (Zech. 4:7), without which the building could never be complete.

When our Lord rose again He commenced to build God's city (Isa. 45:13); He laid the foundation and built His church upon Himself (Mt. 16:18). Christ in resurrection is *"the Living Stone"* (1 Pet. 2:4), to whom we come, and by whom we are built up as "living stones," a "spiritual house, an holy priesthood, to offer up spiritual sacrifices, acceptable to God by Jesus Christ" (1 Pet. 2:4-5).

Israel stumbled over Him because of His poverty and apparent weakness. The lack of expected glory caused Christ to be despised and rejected. He was not the kind of a Saviour Israel looked for and they were offended in Him. He was nevertheless the very One foretold and described. When Israel refused Him and crucified Him, God exalted Him and made Him "the head of the corner." There can be no lasting building without Him. No city, no tower, and no temple will eternally abide that does not have Christ for its stability and for its glory.

Paul, the apostle, preaching in the Jewish synagogue in Antioch of Pisidia showed how the second Psalm foretells the resurrection of Christ. This is what Paul said, "And we declare unto you glad tidings, how that *the promise* which was made unto the fathers, God hath fulfilled the same unto us their children, in that He hath raised up Jesus again; as it is also written in the second Psalm, Thou art My Son, this day have I begotten Thee" (Acts 13:32-33).

In this Messianic Psalm our Lord is seen as raised again to be a King: "Yet have I set My King upon My holy hill of Zion" (Ps. 2:6). Jesus our Lord was raised to reign. He who in death wore the crown of thorns, shall yet wear at Jerusalem the crown as King of kings. He who tasted the deepest shame shall yet know the highest honor in the place where He was crucified.

The Jews rejected the title Pilate wrote on the cross. "Write not, the King of the Jews" they protested, "but that He said, I am King of the Jews" (Jn. 19:21). Pilate would not change the writing, but said, "What I have written, I have written." So the superscription remained as before, *"This is Jesus of Nazareth, the King of the Jews."* Israel gritted their teeth in anger, but the words over the cross of Christ proclaimed the nation's guilt. They crucified their King. But if Israel would not acknowledge her king, God looked down from heaven and said, "Yet have I set My

King upon My holy hill of Zion" (Ps. 2:6).

In resurrection our Lord is King. If not King over us who form the Bride, the church, yet nevertheless King to us. There is no other King but the One who wore the crown of thorns. No other head deserves to wear the crown of glory.

Israel for her blessing waits that day of repentance when she shall say with loud Hosannas to the King, "Blessed is He that cometh in the name of the Lord" (Mt. 21:9). Then shall Jerusalem put on her beautiful garments and know both joy and peace. Then shall be that springtime for the Bridegroom and the Bride when at last the winter will be past and the rain over and gone. Then the flowers will appear on the earth and the time of the singing of the birds will have come. What a Jubilee of Hallelujahs that will be! Then will all Israel sing that psalm of Solomon, resting in peace under His shadow; then shall all oppression be forever past and all the prayers of David the son of Jesse be ended (see Ps. 72).

But there is more. "And as concerning that He raised Him up from the dead, now no more to return to corruption, He said on this wise, I will give you the sure mercies of David" (Acts 13:34). The last sentence of this verse is quoted from Isaiah 55:3. Chapter 55 is one of Isaiah's noted gospel chapters. Like the Lord, it is full of grace and truth. There is water, wine, and milk, for the thirsty and the dying. There is salvation on the easiest possible terms; it is simply to incline the ear and come. There is the promise of every thing new. The sure mercies of David are the gracious gift of God.

Paul, by the Spirit, tells us that these mercies are secured and presented through the resurrection of Christ. It is because God raised Him from the dead that these mercies are possible. They are mercies that are sure upon the faithfulness of God, mercies as great and wonderful as God Himself. They are mercies that should impel us to present ourselves to Him. "I beseech you therefore, brethren, by the mercies of God, that ye present your bodies a living sacrifice, holy, acceptable unto God, which is your reasonable service" (Rom. 12:1).

The whole first eight chapters of the Epistle to the Romans tell the story of these mercies of God. They are bestowed on prodigals. They include the best robe, the ring, the shoes and the fatted calf. The mutual joy of the father and the son begins but never ends. These mercies of God include His loving forgiveness, and His lavish kindness. These mercies in the Epistle to the Romans leave us not only justified and glorified, but children in the bosom of the Father, and joined to Christ as a Bride to a Bridegroom. They tell us of no condemnation and of no separation. They leave us in the wealth of Christ's unmeasured and unwearied love where no enemy will reach us forever. When I read the eighth of Romans, I say with an old farmer I knew, "Ain't them grand words?"

These then are the promises of the Old Testament of Christ's resurrection quoted by Peter and by Paul in the Acts of the Apostles. They tell the reason why He rose again. It was for our sakes He ascended up on high. He opened the path of life. He became a perfect High Priest for the preservation of His people. He brings as a glorious inheritance the sure mercies of David to us. The One who does this is King of kings and Lord of lords forever. He alone is worthy, all honor to His name!

Not only are there New Testament commentaries showing Old Testament promises fulfilled in Christ's resurrection, but the Old Testament is replete with prototypes of this signal event. One of the clearest is in the story of Isaac. As Abraham declares: "I and the lad will go yonder and worship, and come again to you" (Gen. 22:5). What was the ground of such confidence? "By *faith* Abraham offered up Isaac...accounting that God was able to raise him up, even from the dead; from whence also he received him in a figure" (Heb 11:17-19).

In the raising of Isaac "in a figure" there is a type of resurrection securing all the promises of God. Every promise would have failed had Isaac been slain and not raised up again. David, Solomon, Joseph, Mary, Christ, were all of Isaac "according to the flesh." Solomon and Joseph through whom the title descended to Christ; and David and Mary through whom Christ came "according to the flesh," were all the children of Abraham through Isaac.

"In a figure" Isaac died, and "in a figure" Isaac rose again. "After the Spirit" Isaac was Abraham's only son whom he loved. Isaac brightened with hope the future of Abraham even as he filled with joy every passing day. The name Isaac means laughter, and God made both Sarah and Abraham laugh with deep and lasting joy in the possession of Isaac. When Abraham yielded Isaac, he gave his all. Abraham had the honored privilege many generations before Christ of giving a type of the God of all grace who, "so loved the world that He gave His only begotten Son."

The Ark of the Covenant gives another divine illustration. "And the priests that bare the ark of the covenant of the Lord stood firm on dry ground in the midst of Jordan, and all the Israelites passed over on dry ground, until all the people were passed clean over Jordan" (Josh 3:17). "And it came to pass, when all the people were clean passed over, that the ark of the Lord passed over, and the priests in the presence of the people" (Josh. 4:11).

In this type of resurrection, the covenant people were brought into the covenanted inheritance. There everything was new— new food, new experiences, new leadership, new life, and new warfare. The old things of the wilderness were passed away, and in Canaan all things had become new.

The ark went first into the water and remained in its depths "until everything was finished" (Josh. 4:10). The ark coming up out of the waters, after the people had all passed over, gives the type of Christ our Lord dying for us, and also of our dying with Him. "I am crucified with Christ," Paul wrote to the Galatians (2:20). God hath "quickened us together with Christ...and [He] hath raised us up together, and made us sit together in heavenly places in Christ Jesus," the same Paul wrote to the Ephesians (2:5-6). These facts of the death and resurrection of Christ and of our association with Him are beautifully illustrated in the passing of the ark and the people through the Jordan into the land of God's promise. This is the peculiar message of the Epistle to the Ephesians.

Jonah, in sovereign grace is used as a type of Christ and His resurrection not only in spite of his reluctance, but indeed because of it. Running from the Lord, he was intercepted by the divine purpose. "Now the Lord had prepared a great fish to swallow up Jonah. And Jonah was in the belly of the fish three days and three nights" (Jonah 1:17). "And the Lord spake unto the fish, and it vomited out Jonah upon the dry land" (Jonah

2:10). "So Jonah arose, and went unto Nineveh, according to the word of the Lord...So the people of Nineveh believed God" (Jonah 3:3-5).

The Lord's own commentary explains the likeness: "For as Jonas was three days and three nights in the whale's belly; so shall the Son of man be three days and three nights in the heart of the earth" (Mt. 12:40). Thus in the prophet Jonah and what happened to him we have a type of resurrection providing a message and a messenger for Gentiles that mercy might reach them.

The ark which Noah built "to the saving of his house" illustrates another aspect of the resurrection. "And the ark rested in the seventh month, on the seventeenth day of the month, upon the mountains of Ararat" (Gen. 8:4). "And it came to pass in the six hundredth and first year, in the first month, the first day of the month, the waters were dried up from off the earth: and Noah removed the covering of the ark, and looked, and, behold, the face of the ground was dry" (v. 13).

In this type you see resurrection providing rest. The name Noah means rest. Noah (rest) came out of the ark on the day of Christ's resurrection. The ark rested and our Lord rose again on the seventeenth day of the seventh month. So the resting of the ark and the exit of its inhabitants into a new and restored earth were a type and a promise of the new creation from the resurrection of Christ. It was a new beginning in the days of Noah with judgment past and with God's promise for the future. It was a new beginning when our Lord rose again; the beginning of a life which was eternal with blessings that the old creation never could have provided and a promise of security and government that the law never could have guaranteed.

The sheaf of Firstfruits offering is used by Paul to teach the link between Christ's resurrection and the saints'. The Lord instructed His people: "When ye be come into the land which I give unto you, and shall reap the harvest thereof, then ye shall bring a sheaf of the firstfruits of your harvest unto the priest: and he shall wave the sheaf before the Lord, to be accepted for you: on the morrow after the sabbath the priest shall wave it" (Lev. 23:10-11). Paul explains, "But now is Christ risen from the dead, and become the firstfruits of them that slept" (1 Cor.

15:20). He then adds: "Christ the firstfruits, afterward they that are Christ's at His coming" (v. 23).

This sheaf of firstfruits waved before the Lord on the first day of the week was the promise of the coming harvest. It was God's own type of Him who rose early in the morning on the first day of the week. The one sheaf seemed to say, "There is a harvest of others coming just like this one." It was waved before the Lord for His pleasure and delight. That sheaf was the fruit of God's own giving and it was a foretaste of the joy of coming harvest.

The resurrection of Christ is the guarantee of our own resurrection in our own order. The joy of harvest had a triumph all its own; the sheaf of the firstfruits was the herald of this imminent jubilee. The joy in heaven when Christ our Lord ascended there, (Ps. 24:7-8) will be repeated when His people ascend there with Him (Ps. 24:10). This is all one harvest; the sheaf of the firstfruits and the sheaves that follow are all one resurrection accomplishment and glory. Resurrection associates us with Him (Eph. 1:20-2:1) "God raised Him from the dead...and you who were dead in trespasses and sins...hath He raised." Resurrection assures us of being like Him when He comes. "We know that, when He shall appear, we shall be like Him; for we shall see Him as He is" (1 Jn. 3:2).

Thus in type in the Old Testament the story of Christ's resurrection is told. There is a note of triumph, of promise, and joy in all these pictures of His rising from the dead. Before the morning with its singing, there is the long night with its darkness. Before the springtime with its gladness, there is the winter with its coldness and its death. Before the lovely butterfly with its painted wings, there is the crawling caterpillar with its life of lowliness and shame. Before the jubilee with its liberty and blessing, there were the long years of servitude and labor. The weeping endures for the night, but joy cometh in the morning. He who is "the resurrection and the life" will dry all tears and drive all sickness and death far away. The feast with the resurrected Lazarus and his friends sitting at the table with Him will never end. The fragments of that feasting will never be gathered, for the fullness of His royal bounty will never be depleted. "So shall we ever be with the Lord" (1 Thess. 4:17).

130

CHAPTER TEN

Despising His Renown

"And I took unto me two staves; the one I called Beauty, and the other I called Bands; and I fed the flock...And I took my staff, even Beauty, and cut it asunder, that I might break my covenant which I had made with all the people. And it was broken in that day: and so the poor of the flock that waited upon me knew that it was the word of the Lord. And I said unto them, If ye think good, give me my price; and if not, forbear. So they weighed for my price thirty pieces of silver. And the Lord said unto me, Cast it unto the potter: a goodly price that I was prized at of them. And I took the thirty pieces of silver, and cast them to the potter in the house of the Lord. Then I cut asunder mine other staff, even Bands, that I might break the brotherhood between Judah and Israel" (Zech. 11:7, 10-14).

Beauty and Bands were the names on the two staves of the Shepherd Prophet when he fed the flock of God. The fact that the prophet had two staves instead of the common one would arrest attention. When the names on the staves were observed, the people would know that this equipment contained a prophetic communication. They would know it all meant something, but what it did mean was a mystery till all was explained.

First, the staff Beauty, and then the staff Bands, were broken. Between these two breakings the price of the Shepherd is asked for and given—thirty pieces of silver. The comment of the Shepherd Himself on this disgusting valuation is the nearest to sarcasm from His lips in the Scriptures: *"A goodly price that I was prized at of them."* Casting the silver down in the house of the Lord is a gesture of abhorrent disapproval of the transaction.

This is the incident between the breaking of the two staves. On the breaking of the staff Beauty, the covenant of blessing from which Israel derived all her loveliness was completely destroyed (see Ezek. 16:13-14). When the staff Bands was broken, the unity and loving fellowship between the people were gone (see Ps. 133:1-3). In between breaking the staves is the weighing for His worth the price of a common slave.

This dramatic method of teaching the truth of God in that distant period of the past was common in bringing prophetic messages from heaven. The message of this whole matter is as simple as it is profound. Simple for the poor to see and understand; profound for the wise to ponder and search for deeper counsel.

It was the utter lack of appreciation of the worth and work of the Shepherd that caused the loss to Israel of all that was lovely toward God, and of all that was so good and pleasant among His people. *"A goodly price that I was prized at of them!"*

Thirty pieces of silver, for the Lord of Life they gave;
Thirty pieces of silver—only the price of a slave! (William Blane)

Yes, thirty pieces of silver was the stipulated compensation for a slave (Ex. 21:32). This was the very least value that could be set on the head of a human being. This act of callous blindness, putting the lowest price on the priceless love and service of the Best of heaven, was the calm and unnoticed act that blighted every beauty and every blessing of the favored people.

A choice that is made with little thought or exercise often manifests where the heart is. Judas thought so little of the thirty pieces of silver that he could actually kiss His Master with them already in his bag. It was these thirty pieces of silver marked Judas out as a despiser of God's Christ, and a traitor. Accept the price of a slave for the Shepherd of the Sheep? Judas did it. The merest speck of true love would have scorned such a valuation.

It was the price of His worth in the minds of the priests as well. The stirring of indignation is readily seen in the holy sarcasm of the words, *"A goodly price that I was prized at of them."* The loathing of the money is seen in casting the pieces to the potter in the house of the Lord. Let the potter put the silver of the wretched bargain with the shards of his broken and worthless vessels. This was what was done with the price of blood, the price of His blood. The potter's field was purchased to bury strangers in (Mt. 27:3-10). Here the potter had sown the wreckage of his ruined work; in the field so full of broken, hardened clay, the irretrievable destruction of marred vessels; there amid the scattered remnants of spoiled pottery they bought a place, with Israel's price of His blood; a place to bury strangers in.

To Israel, the world is still the potter's field. The wreckage of Abraham's people—broken, hard and dry—is everywhere. Every nation is another potter's field. There are no vessels unto honor there now, nothing in the potter's field sanctified and meet for the Master's use. In this hopeless potter's field the dying sons of Israel are buried. They are strangers from their land, and from their inheritance. They are strangers still, in the countries of their adoption and supposed citizenship. Worst of all, they are strangers to grace and to God. The price of His blood has been cast to the potter, in the house of the Lord. The vessel of the nation, and the vessels of the persons who comprise the nation, have been molded by the potter, by that most dreadful transaction at Jerusalem, nearly two millenia ago. The prophet said it should be so, and it was, and is so still.

What greater sin could any saint commit than to put a shameful price on the Shepherd or His work? To prefer another to Christ; to accept the price of fleshly gratification instead of the priceless Saviour, is an insult of which only love can feel the enormity. If our lives reveal that silver is more to us than Christ, what a tremendous sin this is! If the world be gain to me, then Christ is sold again.

What made Paul such a great man was not his talents, or his gifts; but the fact that he actually counted all things but loss for the excellency of the knowledge of Christ Jesus his Lord. To Paul there was no worth outside of his Master. It was not merely that Christ had the higher value. The world and all it had to offer, for pride or pleasure, was dung. All Paul could see before him for ambition, or attainment, was Christ. All Paul could see around him was Christ in His people, or Christ in the gospel. Paul put the value where the value belonged.

Judas knew a great deal about Christ, but Judas did not value Christ. Do we value Him? Do we value His shepherd care? Do we put the right worth on His companionship? Do we count conformity to Christ to be the spirit of Christianity? Can we say, "To me to live is Christ"? If not, this is the reason the Beauty and the Bands are gone. This is the reason the lovely things of the Spirit are lacking in His vineyard. This is one of the main causes of discord among brethren. The staff Bands is broken because He is despised. Devotedness to Christ is the cementing tie that binds saints to each other. Probably the deep, deep secret of all the famine and desolation of this Laodicean day is the lost consciousness of the priceless value of our Immanuel.

Israel's way of recovery is also the way for us. That recovery is pictured in Zechariah's next chapter: "And I will pour upon the house of David and upon the inhabitants of Jerusalem, the spirit of grace and of supplications; and they shall look upon Me, whom they have pierced, and they shall mourn for Him, as one mourneth for his only son, and shall be in bitterness for Him, as one that is in bitterness for his firstborn" (Zech. 12:10).

It is that look into the heart of God that brings true repentance, to think that my coldness to Christ has wounded the heart of God. When the Lord turned and looked on Peter, Peter was at that moment looking on the Lord. Their eyes met, and Peter saw more than the face of his Master; he saw into His wounded heart. This look led to Peter's repentance and restoration.

May we look again upon Him whom we pierced. Let us confess our sin. Let us repent of our senseless and base folly. Thirty pieces of silver instead of Christ! Let us say, "Take the world but give me Jesus." Let us hate as sin and wickedness every supplanting object, or ambition, that would obscure Christ from our vision. May we live "not unto ourselves but unto Him who died for us and rose again." Then it will be: "Nevertheless I live, yet not I, but Christ liveth in me." Then the gathering together of God's saints will be like Jerusalem, where God is known in her palaces for a refuge; a city beautiful for situation, the joy of the whole district. Others will exclaim, "Behold, how good and how pleasant it is for brethren to dwell together in unity." The Great Shepherd of the sheep will feed the poor of His flock, with unbroken staves, Beauty and Bands, in His wise and able hands. "Happy is that people, that is in such a case; yea, happy is that people, whose God is the Lord" (Ps. 144:15).

CHAPTER ELEVEN

His Coming Again

No sooner did our Lord leave this earth for heaven than a message was sent to the disciples as they still gazed upward where they had seen Him disappear. It was a message of His coming back again. "Two men," evidently angelic messengers, stood by the disciples, as they wonderingly gazed toward heaven. This is what these messengers said, "Ye men of Galilee, why stand ye gazing up into heaven? This same Jesus, which is taken up from you into heaven, shall so come in like manner as ye have seen Him go into heaven" (Acts 1:11).

Angels usually call Him Lord. Yet when He ascended in glory the angels say, "This same Jesus." Now that our Lord has gone to heaven, clothed with all the majesty that rightly belongs to Him, our God does not want us to think that He is not still the same as when He walked the roads of Judea and Galilee, dispensing mercy and healing everywhere. Though shining with a glory above the brightness of the sun, He is the very same Saviour as when He sat on Sychar's well.

John, who leaned on Jesus' bosom, has not lost the Friend with a tender heart. Thomas who said, "My Lord, and my God," could still look for Him who said, "Reach hither thy finger and behold My hands, and reach hither thy hand and thrust it into My side, and be not faithless but believing" (Jn. 20:27). Peter, who held Him by the feet, and who said, "Lord, to whom shall we go? Thou hast the words of eternal life" (Jn. 6:68), will see that same blessed Saviour unchanged in the glory. Lazarus, who sat at the table with Him, and Zacchaeus of the sycamore tree can look for the very same Jesus to come back again. And Mary, who sat at His feet, will enjoy such a place forever.

The words of the angels would impress the hearts of each of the disciples with the precious fact that the one they had known would be eternally the same. None of them had lost the Saviour who spoke peace to their hearts. Not one had lost the Friend who so tenderly cared for him. It would have been so natural for all the disciples to feel that their exalted Lord, so marvelously transported to heaven, would not be the same as when He fed them with loaves and fishes in the wilderness.

The One whom Magdalene called "Rabboni" (Jn. 20:16), was coming again, her unchanged and gracious Lord. He whose voice had so often stilled the fears of His troubled disciples, as He spoke peace or pardon to their hearts, was coming back again. There was unmeasured consolation to the wondering "men of Galilee," when the angels assured them that He who was in heaven, and He who was returning for them again, was the same Jesus. How marvellous that the Christ of the Glory is the Christ of the carpenter shop! How transcendently precious that the Christ of Bethesda, and of Sychar's well, is still the very same. He has the same love, the same longsuffering, the same goodness, though now He sits on the throne of God. The One who cheered us on our pathway, the One who cared for us as a Shepherd for His sheep, is coming back again.

And He will come "in like manner" as He went. Our Lord went away, "while they beheld"; when He returns "we shall see Him as He is" (1 Jn. 3:2). With their own eyes they gazed intently upon Him as He went up; with our own eyes we shall see Him without a veil between, when He comes again. "A cloud received Him out of their sight" (Acts 1:9). It will be a cloud that will bring Him back to this earth as well: "Behold, He cometh with clouds; and every eye shall see Him" (Rev. 1:7).

We read, *And when He had spoken these things* (Acts 1:9). He talked with them as He left them, and how sweet will be His voice when we hear it audibly for the first time:

"Oh, the blessed joy of meeting, all the desert past!
Oh, the wondrous words of greeting, He shall speak at last!
He and I in that bright glory, one deep joy shall share,
Mine to be forever with Him, His that I am there."

The most thrilling joy of the present moment for the people of

God, is, "The coming of the Lord draweth nigh" (Jas. 5:8). Any one of these days we may see Him. The tokens of "the promise of His coming" are multiplied. The Spirit of God is witnessing that our "redemption draweth nigh"; may we be watching for Him.

There is not a more striking sign of the nearness of the coming of our Lord than that of the reviving of *Magen David*, the star (or shield) of David by the Jews everywhere, even by the nation of Israel in their land. The star of David has been chiseled by the Jews over hundreds of their synagogues; it has been printed on millions of their magazines and publications; and it now appears as the outstanding symbol on the flag of the new nation of Israel. A regiment of Jews under General Allenby carried this six-pointed star at their head as they marched as victors into the city of Jerusalem in 1917, when the Turks surrendered to its liberators.

This so-called "Star of David" is the symbol on the scepter of Judah, and is the insignia of the coming King. It is the star of Shiloh. The hidden wonders of that star are so remarkable that it seems likely it had its origin with God.

Like the ark of the covenant in the tabernacle, this six-pointed star of David is a perfect witness to the person of Christ. A more complete and striking symbol of Christ in such a simple form as this hexagram could not be conceived. The figure is so plain and simple that it is easily understood. Undoubtedly the Lord intended this star to be a prophecy of Christ as He is revealed in the Scripture, and this it is in a remarkable way.

The star of David is formed by combining two equilateral triangles. These triangles are not laid one upon the other, but so combined that they could not be separated. If you will examine the lines of these triangles you will notice that when the line of the first triangle passes over the line of the second triangle in this place, it passes under it in the next. Thus, although the two triangles maintain their individual completeness, they are so interwoven that they form one complete unity, and that unity is a star. In every representation of this star the complete lines of the two triangles are kept.

This hexagram, formed of two equilateral triangles, is a two-fold trinity in unity. Perfect trinity in unity could not be more clearly expressed than by an equilateral triangle. The three sides and the three angles of this triangle are equal, and the figure is one. With two of these triangles combined in such a way that they could not be separated, you have the idea of a two-fold trinity in one perfect union.

This six-pointed star is sometimes referred to as "Solomon's Seal." Although adopted as the superstitious hexagram of the Greeks, it was the insignia on the scepter of Judah long before.

The Scriptures of the Old Testament and the Gospels of the New Testament writers unite their testimony in revealing that the Messiah of Israel, the man Christ Jesus, was true God and also very man. In the name of Messiah in Isaiah 9:6 you have the fullness of Deity in three persons ascribed to a Man. "And His name shall be called Wonderful, Counselor, the Mighty God, the Everlasting Father, the Prince of Peace." This is the name of Him 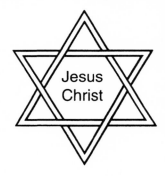 who was a "child born" and a "son given." This is the name of "the Father, and of the Son, and of the Holy Ghost." It is the one name of the Trinity in unity. It is the name of the Man Christ Jesus. Thomas called Him, "my Lord and my God." Nathanael said to Him, "Rabbi, Thou art the Son of God; Thou art the King of Israel." The Scriptures reveal that, although the Deity exists in three Persons, the fullness of Godhead belongs to each. This is a deep and exalted mystery, too eternally infinite for our limited comprehension. We worship at the footstool of His greatness as we lean upon the love of His heart.

I could not conceive of so simple a figure to convey the truth of this trinity in unity in the Godhead of Christ as the equilateral triangle. Three straight lines are the least that can enclose a space, and they form the strongest geometric figure. The absolute Godhead of Christ not only encloses all that is to be held for God in heaven and in earth, but it is this infinite power and majesty that encircles and holds forever a poor trembling sinner like me.

The true and perfect manhood of Christ is also a trinity in unity. Even in death this was seen. Christ our Lord bore our sins "in His own *body* on the tree." At Calvary He "poured out His *soul* unto death." His last words on the cross were, "Father, into Thy hands I commend My *spirit*." Our Lord had "spirit, soul, and body." That perfect body, that holy soul, that constant spirit; how could they be better expressed than by three equal and straight lines? These three joined lines form the other equilateral triangle. When you consider these two facts of our Lord's exalted person, His perfect Deity and His holy humanity, united forever in the Man Christ Jesus, what a striking suggestion of these revelations you have in the union of two equilateral triangles!

Then, when these united triangles form a star, what a symbol of the truth of God that this One is the only hope of Israel or of the church! Some years ago, President Benes of Czechoslovakia said in a speech given at Cleveland, Ohio, "I cannot see a single star of hope on the international horizon." He did not look high enough. Had Mr. Benes listened, he might have heard One say, "I am the root and the offspring of David, and the bright and Morning Star." There is no other star of hope but Christ. He is the bright, and only hope of the future. If there is to be blessing in earth or heaven, it must come from Him.

How tragic to see Israel rallying around this star, while hating still the One whom that star so clearly represents! Israel is now a nation in its own land. They proudly carry their flag with the Star of Shiloh prominent upon it, but, like Joseph's brethren, they know not the glory of the One they hated long ago. They do not know that the One they rejected is their only hope in the crisis that is coming. Blindly the guilty nation confesses that Shiloh is their only hope for the future, but they reject the fact of His Deity, to which the star bears witness. They will never know peace till they worship at His feet.

The last "I am's" of our Lord in the book of Revelation show that He is indeed the One to whom the star bears tribute. He said, "I am Alpha and Omega, the beginning and the end, the first and the last." Our Lord was the Alpha of God's revelation; He was the Beginning of God's creation; and before all this He was the First. This is the one trinity of the past. He is the Omega of God's words—the conclusion of all God has to say; He is the

End of God's creation—the completer of the last of God's great works; and after all this He shall be the Last. These form a twofold trinity in unity. These six supreme attributes and characteristics belong to Him. He is the fullness of revelation in the past and in the future. He is the Mighty God of all creation. He is the eternally existing One, the same yesterday, today, and forever. He is Jehovah, who is, who was, and who is to come, the Almighty.

This is the One who says in verse 16 of the last chapter of the Bible, "I Jesus...am the root and the offspring of David, and the bright and morning star." The living root in the ground is the hope of all that grows on the earth. The Morning Star heralds the coming day when the darkness shall be past and the true light shine forever. The hope of the future is this bright Star of the Heavens who was once without form and comeliness as a root out of dry ground. May our hearts say with devoted John, "Even so, come, Lord Jesus."

Think briefly with me concerning His name. Isaiah declares: "For unto us a child is born; unto us a son is given; and the government shall be upon His shoulder; and His name shall be called Wonderful, Counselor, the Mighty God, the Everlasting Father, the Prince of Peace" (Isa. 9:6). This is the first intimation of the truth of John 3:16. It was God's grace that sent Christ, but it was God's love that gave Him. He was not only a Saviour sent; He was a Son given.

And His name! What a name! "Wonderful, Counselor, The Mighty God, The Everlasting Father, The Prince of Peace." This is His Name upon whose shoulder the government of the universe rests. This is the Name of the Prince of Peace. When the great plans of God's glorious working were made, He was the Counselor; when the stupendous acts of creation, redemption, and resurrection were to be performed, He was The Mighty God who wrought it all. The ages and their revelations are begotten of Him, for He is the Father of Eternity. This is the inconceivable glory of Him who came from heaven to earth. It is the fullest possible expression of Deity. This is God in all the effulgence of His glory. The Prince of Peace is He who hides in His person all the fullness of the Godhead bodily, for He is God!

This threefold declaration of the name of the Prince of

Peace—Counselor, The Mighty God, The Everlasting Father, is not all of this name. There is still the name "Wonderful" preceding this threefold revelation of Himself. This word "Wonderful" is elsewhere translated "secret" (Jud. 13:18). This suggests that after all that is known of His name by His works of creation or redemption, there are heights and depths of knowledge of this One that can never be revealed; His name is Secret. The only reason His name is Secret is because it is Wonderful, that is, so full of wonder that we cannot comprehend it. God has held nothing back from us. In Christ God has told us all. "The only begotten Son, which is in the bosom of the Father, He hath declared Him" (Jn. 1:18). His name is secret only because of our limitations. The ages of ages will forever be unfolding God. How marvelous that One so infinitely glorious should be for sinners the Prince of Peace!

Why is He called the Prince of Peace? Because in His reign there will be abundance of peace as long as the moon endureth (Ps. 72:7); because He at last will speak peace to the heathen (Zech. 9:10); because He broke down the middle wall of partition between Jew and Gentile, so making peace (Eph. 2:14-15); and because He made peace by the blood of His cross (Col. 1:20), when the chastisement was upon Him (Isa. 53:5). His own feet were beautiful, bringing the gospel of peace to men, and He sent His servants to preach peace in His Name. The fruit of His Spirit is peace. When He came in resurrection to His disciples, His first word was "peace." When He left them with the priestly benediction, as His hands were uplifted at Bethany, His last word was "peace." "The Lord bless thee and keep thee: the Lord make His face to shine upon thee, and be gracious unto thee: the Lord lift up His countenance upon thee and give thee peace" (Num. 6:24-25).

In that coming blissful jubilee the name of Israel's King will be "Prince of Peace." No prince or king has ever yet deserved that title. It does not belong to the warriors of the earth. They usually lead nations that delight in war. But Christ is and shall be Prince of Peace. He stands alone, exalted and supreme, the object of reverence and worship from angels and from men. He is not next to God; He is God Himself. There is nothing of God that is not comprehended in this marvelous name given to the child born and to the Son given.

And He is given "unto us." The grace is as mighty as the Person Himself. Had this majestic fact of incarnation been only for our knowledge and observation, it would have been wonderful indeed. But it was "unto us" wholly. It was for our redemption and eternal blessing that this One with His great name came down to be born and to be the Prince of Peace. He was born for us. He was given for us. He is what He is *for us!* He is God for us, to be a mighty Saviour. He is Man for us, to have a heart of loving sympathy.

There is a tenderness from the heart of God, as well as power from the throne of God, in the message of Isaiah 9:6. Thank God it was "unto us" the child was born, and "unto us" the Son was given. Thank God the angels' message at Bethlehem was: "Unto you is born this day in the city of David a Saviour, which is Christ the Lord." Thank God that "unto them that look for Him shall He appear the second time." Maranatha!

Names & Titles of Christ

Adam, the Last (1 Cor. 15:45)
Advocate (1 Jn. 2:1)
All & in All (Col. 3:11)
Almighty (Rev. 1:8)
Altogether Lovely One? (Song of Sol. 5:16)
Amen (Rev. 3:14)
Anchor (Heb. 6:19)
Ancient of Days (Dan. 7:9-11 with Rev. 1:13-16)
Angel [of the Lord] (Gen. 16:9-14?; Gen. 48:16?)
Anointed, His (Ps. 2:2). See also *Messiah.*
Apostle (Heb. 3:1)
Arm of the Lord (Isa. 53:1)
Author—and Finisher of faith (Heb. 12:2)
        —of eternal salvation (Heb. 5:9)
Alpha & Omega (Rev. 1:8; 21:6)
Balm of Gilead? (Jer. 8:22)
Beginning (Col. 1:18)
        —of the creation of God (Rev. 3:14)
        —and the end[ing] (Rev. 1:8; 21:6; 22:13)
Begotten
        —First B. of the Dead (Rev. 1:5)
        —Only B.
                —of the Father (Jn. 1:14)
                —Son [of God] (Jn. 3:16; 1 Jn. 4:9). See also *Son.*
Beloved (Eph. 1:6)
        —Son (2 Pet. 1:17). See also *Son.*

Bishop of your souls (1 Pet. 2:25)
Blessed and only Potentate (1 Tim. 6:15)
Branch (Isa. 11:1; Jer. 23:5; Zech. 3:8; 6:12; Rev. 11:1)
Bread   —B. from heaven (Jn. 6:32, 41, 50)
        —B. of God (Jn. 6:33)
        —B. of life (Jn. 6:35)
        —living B. (Jn. 6:51)
        —true B. (Jn. 6:32, 35)
Bridegroom (Mt. 9:15; Jn. 3:29; Rev. 21:9)
Bright & Morning Star, see *Star*.
Brightness of His (God's) glory (Heb. 1:3)
Captain of their salvation (Heb. 2:12; Josh. 5:4?)
Carpenter['s son] (Mt. 13:55; Mk. 6:3)
Chief[est among ten thousand?] Song of Sol. 5:10)
        —C. Corner Stone (Eph. 2:20; 1 Pet. 2:6). See also *Stone*.
        —C. Shepherd (1 Pet. 5:4). See also *Shepherd*.
Child, [the young] (Isa. 9:6; Mt. 2:8-21)
        —C. Jesus (Lk. 2:27, 43)
        —holy C. Jesus (Acts 4:27, 30)
Chosen of God (Lk. 23:35)
Christ (Mt. 1:17; Mk. 8:29; Jn. 1:41; Rom. 1:16; 1 Cor. 1:23)
        —C. of God (Jn. 12:34)
        —Jesus C. (Mt. 1:1; Phil. 1:6; 2 Tim. 2:3)
              —J. C. the righteous (1 Jn. 2:1)
              —His Son J. C. (1 Jn. 5:20)
              —our Saviour J. C. (2 Tim. 1:10)
        —C. Jesus [our Lord] (Col. 1:28; 1 Thess. 1:12)
        —Lord [and Saviour] Jesus C. (2 Pet. 2:20; Rev. 22:21)
Comforter (Isa. 61:2; Jn. 14:16)
Commander (Isa. 55:4)
Consolation of Israel (Lk. 2:25)
Corn of Wheat (Jn. 12:24)
Cornerstone (Eph. 2:20; see also Isa. 28:16)
Counsellor (Isa. 9:6; Isa. 40:13?)
Covert (Isa. 32:2)
Creator of all things (Col. 1:16)
Daysman? (Job 9:33)
Dayspring from on high (Lk. 1:78)
Day Star (2 Pet. 1:19). See also *Bright & Morning Star*.

Deliverer (Rom. 11:26)
Desire of all nations (Hag. 2:7)
Door [of the sheepfold] (Jn. 10:7, 9)
Emmanuel (Mt. 1:23; see also Isa. 7:14; 8:8)
End, see *Beginning & the End.*
End of the Law (Rom 10:4)
Express image of His (God's) person (Heb. 1:3)
Faithful Witness (Rev. 1:5; 3:14; 19:11)
Faithful & True (Rev. 19:11)
Father of Eternity (Isa. 9:6)
Fellow of God? (Zech. 13:7)
First & the Last (Rev. 1:17)
First begotten of the dead (Rev. 1:5)
Firstborn
  —F. among many brethren (Rom. 8:29)
  —F. of every creature (Col. 1:15)
  —F. from the dead (Col. 1:18)
Firstfruits [of them that slept] (1 Cor. 15:20, 23)
Foundation (Isa. 28:16; 1 Cor. 3:11)
Fountain (Jer. 2:13?; Zech. 13:1)
Forerunner (Heb. 6:20)
Friend of sinners (Mt. 11:19; Lk. 7:34)
Fulness of the Godhead (Col. 2:9)
Gift of God (Jn. 4:10; 2 Cor. 9:15)
Glory of God (Isa. 60:1)
God (Jn. 1:1; Mt. 1:23; Rom. 9:5; 1 Tim. 3:16; Heb. 1:8)
  —Bread of G. (Jn. 6:33)
  —Chosen of G. (Lk. 23:35)
  —Christ of G. (Jn. 12:34)
  —Gift of G. (2 Cor. 9:15)
  —Glory of G. (Isa. 60:1)
  —G. my Saviour (Lk. 1:47)
  —the Mighty G. (Isa. 9:6)
  —my G. (Jn. 20:28)
Good Master (Mt. 19:16)
Governor (Mt. 2:6)
Great High Priest (Heb. 4:14)
Greater than...
  —Abraham (Jn. 8:53)

—Jacob (Jn. 4:12)
—John the Baptist (Mt. 11:11)
—Jonah (Mt. 12:41)
—the temple (Mt. 12:6)
—Solomon (Lk. 11:31)
Guide (Ps. 48:14)
Head (even Christ) (Eph. 4:15)
—H. of all principality & power (Col. 2:10)
—H. of the Body, the Church (Col. 1:18)
—H. of every man (1 Cor. 11:3)
—H. of the corner (Ps. 118:22; Mt. 21:42)
Heir of all things (Heb. 1:2)
Helper (Heb. 13:6)
Hiding Place (Isa. 32:2)
High Priest (Heb. 3:1; 7:1)
Holy Child (Acts 4:30)
Holy One [& the Just] (Acts 2:27; 3:14)
—H. of God (Mk. 1:24)
—H. of Israel (Isa. 41:14)
Hope of Israel? (Jer. 17:3)
Horn of salvation (Ps. 18:2; Lk. 1:69)
I AM (Jn. 8:24, 58)
—I am the Bread of Life (Jn. 6:35).
—I am the Light of the World (Jn. 9:5).
—I am the Good Shepherd (Jn. 10:11).
—I am the Door (Jn. 10:9).
—I am the Resurrection & the Life (Jn. 11:25).
—I am the true Vine (Jn. 15:1)
—I am the Way (Jn. 14:6).
Image of [the invisible] God (2 Cor. 4:4; Col. 1:15)
Intercessor (Heb. 7:25)
Jehovah (Isa. 26:4; 40:3)
Jesus (Mt. 1:21)
—J. Christ [the Son of God] (Heb. 13:9; Jn. 20:31)
—J. [Christ] of Nazareth (Acts 4:10; 22:8)
—J. the King (Mt. 26:36)
Judge (Micah 5:1; Acts 10:42)
—Righteous J. (2 Tim. 4:8)
Just One (Acts 7:52)

King (Zech. 14:16)
        —K. of the daughter of Zion (Jn. 12:15)
        —K. of glory (Ps. 24:10)
        —K. of Israel (Mt. 27:42; Jn. 1:49)
        —K. of the Jews (Mt. 2:2; Mk. 15:2; Jn. 19:19)
        —K. of kings (Rev. 17:14; 19:16)
        —K. of peace (Heb. 7:2)
        —K. of righteousness (Heb. 7:2)
        —K. of saints (Rev. 15:3)
Kinsman? (Ruth 2:14)
Lamb [of God] (Jn. 1:29, 36; 1 Pet 1:19; Rev. 5:6, 12; 7:17)
Last, see *First*.
Lawgiver (Isa. 33:22)
Life (1 Jn. 1:2)
        —Eternal L. [which was with the Father] (1 Jn. 1:2; 5:20)
        —Word of L. (1 Jn. 1:1)
Light (Jn. 12:35)
        —great L. (Isa. 9:2)
        —L. to lighten Gentiles (Isa. 42:6; Lk. 2:32)
        —L. of men (Jn. 1:4)
        —L. of the world (Jn. 9:25)
        —true L. (Jn. 1:9)
Lion of the tribe of Judah (Rev. 5:5)
Lord [& Saviour] (1 Cor. 12:3; 2 Pet. 1:11), see also *Master*.
        —L. of [over] all (Acts 10:36; Rom. 10:12)
        —L. of both the dead & the living (Rom. 14:9)
        —L. of glory (1 Cor. 2:8). See also *Glory* and *Brightness*.
        —L. of lords (Rev. 19:16)
        —One L. (Eph. 4:5)
        —L. of Peace (2 Thess. 3:16)
        —L. of the harvest (Mt. 9:38)
        —L. of the Sabbath (Lk. 6:5)
Man (Jn. 19:5; Acts 17:31; 1 Tim. 2:5). See also *Son of Man*.
        —M. of Sorrows (Isa. 53:3)
        —M. Christ Jesus (1 Tim 2:5)
        —Second M. (1 Cor. 15:47)
        —Son of M. (Mk. 10:33)
Master (Mt. 8:19)—*the translation of seven Greek words:*
        —Kurios (Mk. 13:35; Eph. 6:9), often trans. Lord; owner

—Despotes (2 Tim. 2:21), owner but emphasizes power
—Oikodespotes (Mt. 10:25; Lk. 13:25), master of a house
—Epistates (Lk. 5:5; 8:24, 45; 9:33), commander
—Didaskalos (Mt. 8:19; 12:38; 22:16), teacher
—Kathegetes (Mt. 23:8, 10), guide or leader
—Rabbi [Rabboni] (Jn. 1:29, 49), Heb. [Aram.] teacher
Mediator (1 Tim. 2:5)
Merciful High Priest (Heb. 2:17)
Mercy Seat (Rom. 3:24-25)
Messiah (Dan. 9:25; Jn. 1:41; 4:25)
Mighty God (Isa. 9:6; 63:1)
Minister of the Sanctuary (Heb. 8:2)
Nazarene (Mk. 1:24)
Nobleman (Lk. 19:12)
Offering (Eph. 5:2; Heb. 10:10)
Offspring of David (Rev. 22:16). See also *Root.*
Ointment poured forth (Song of Sol. 1:3)
Omega. See *Alpha & Omega.*
Only begotten Son, see *Son.*
Passover (1 Cor. 5:7)
Peace, our (Eph. 2:14)
Physician (Mt. 9:12; Lk. 4:23)
Plant of Renown (Ezek. 34:29)
Potentate, Blessed and only, see *Blessed*
Prince [& a Saviour] (Acts 3:15; 5:31)
        —P. of Peace (Isa. 9:6; 2 Thess. 3:16)
        —P. of the kings of the earth (Rev. 1:5)
Prophet (Acts 3:22-23)
        —Great P. (Lk. 7:16; 24:19)
        —P. of Nazareth (Mt. 21:11)
Propitiation (1 Jn. 2:2; 4:10)
Power of God (1 Cor. 1:24)
Priest (Heb. 4:14)
Quickening (life-giving) Spirit (1 Cor. 15:45)
Rabbi (Jn. 3:2; Mt. 26:25; Jn. 20:16)
Ransom (1 Tim. 2:6)
Redeemer, Redemption (Isa. 59:20; 60:16; 1 Cor. 1:30)
Refuge (Isa. 25:4)
Resurrection & the Life (Jn. 11:25)

Righteousness (Jer. 23:6; 33:16; 1 Cor. 1:30)
Rock [of offence] (Deut. 32:15; 1 Cor. 10:4; Rom. 9:33; 1 Pet. 2:8)
Rod (Isa. 11:1)
Root   —R. of David (Rev. 22:16)
          —R. out of a dry ground (Isa. 53:2)
Rose of Sharon? (Song of Sol. 2:1)
Sacrifice (Eph. 5:2)
Same, the (Heb. 1:12)
Sanctification (1 Cor. 1:30)
Saviour [of the world] (Lk. 1:47; 2:11; 1 Jn. 4:14)
Second Man, see *Man.*
Seed of Abraham (Gal. 3:16, 19)
Seed   —S. of Abraham (Gal. 3:16, 19)
          —S. of David (2 Tim. 2:8)
          —S. of the woman (Gen. 3:15)
Servant (Isa. 42:1; 49:5-7; Mt. 12:18)
Shadow of a great Rock (Isa. 32:2)
Shepherd
          —S. & Bishop of souls (1 Pet. 2:25)
          —Chief S. (1 Pet. 5:4)
          —Good S. (Jn. 10:11, 14)
          —Great S. (Heb. 13:20)
Shiloh (Gen. 49:10)
Son (Isa. 9:6; 1 Jn. 4:14)
          —of Abraham (Mt. 1:1)
          —S. of David (Mt. 9:27; 15:22; 20:30; Mk. 10:46-47)
          —S. of [the living] God (Mt. 4:3, 6; 16:16; Jn 9:35; 10:36)
                   —His dear S. (or the S. of His love) (Col. 1:13)
                   —His own S. (Rom. 8:32)
                   —My [Beloved] Son (Ps. 2:7; Mt. 17:5;
                   —only begotten S. [of God] (Jn. 1:18; 3:16, 18)
                   —S. of the Blessed (Mk. 14:61)
                   —S. of the Highest [Most High] (Mk. 5:7)
                   —S. of the Father (2 Jn. 3)
          —of Joseph (as was supposed) (Jn. 1:45)
          —S. of Man (Mt. 16:27; 20:28; Lk. 6:5)
          —S. of Mary (Mk. 6:3)
Sower (Mt. 13:37)
Star   —Bright & Morning S. (Rev. 22:16)

—S. out of Jacob (Num. 24:17)

Stone   —Chief corner S., elect, precious (Eph. 2:20; 1 Pet. 2:6)

       —living S. (1 Pet. 2:4)

       —S. of stumbling (1 Pet. 2:8)

Sun of Righteousness (Mal. 4:2)

Surety (Heb. 7:22)

Teacher (Mt. 26:18; Jn. 3:2; 11:28). See also *Master.*

Tender Plant (Isa. 53:2)

Testator (Heb. 9:15-17)

True Bread, see *Bread.*

Truth (Jn. 14:6)

Vine (Jn. 15:1, 5)

Way (Jn. 14:6)

Wisdom [of God] (1 Cor. 1:24, 30)

Wonderful (Isa. 9:6)

Word (Jn. 1:1)

       —W. of God (Rev. 19:13)

       —W. of Life (1 Jn. 1:1)

Scripture Index

Printed in the United Kingdom
by Lightning Source UK Ltd.
121015UK00001B/137